My Amazing Journey of Faith

Memoirs of the Extraordinary
Life and Ministry of Pastor
Emma Loretta Curry Creamer

BARBARA WAY WASHINGTON

WestBow
PRESS
A DIVISION OF THOMAS NELSON

WestBow Press
A Division of Thomas Nelson
1663 Liberty Drive
Bloomington, IN 47403
www.westbowpress.com
1-(866) 928-1240

ISBN: 978-1-4497-9630-3 (sc)
ISBN: 978-1-4497-9631-0 (hc)
ISBN: 978-1-4497-9629-7 (e)
Library of Congress Control Number: 2013909599

Printed in the United States of America.

WestBow Press rev. date: 7/12/2013

DEDICATION

With enduring gratitude, I dedicate this book to those who made significant contributions to my life at the times of my greatest need.

First, my mother, the late *Olive M. Curry*, who taught me how to overcome low self-esteem while at the same time teaching me obedience and truthfulness, and most importantly how to love God. There was no better mother than she was, and nobody loved God more than she did. By the world's standards, she didn't have much, but by heaven's, she had it all. Her rich faith and trust in God made each one of my siblings and I people of faith who love God, trust God, and take God at His word.

The late *Mother Daisy Moore*, one of the church mothers at Gethsemane Church of God in Christ in Altoona, Pennsylvania. Mother Moore believed in me when I was nine years old and spoke about God's hand upon me even as a little girl. I will always cherish Mother Moore's words to me as she told me I had "a calling" on my life.

My former pastor, the late *Reverend Ross B. Rainey*, who taught me how to stand firm in hard times and trust God, regardless of the circumstances. Reverend Rainey told me to look above the visible and see God's word so that I might be a minister who finishes strong. He helped me tremendously and encouraged me to be steadfast and unmovable and to always abound in the work of the Lord.

The late *Dr. L. Ramona Howard*, my faithful friend for 36 years with a Ph.D. in Psychology, who taught me how to be real, how to enjoy the ministry, and how to speak with clarity so that I might be a shepherd who never fails to encourage the sheep. For her friendship, I will always be grateful.

Bishop J. Delano Ellis, II of Cleveland, Ohio, Senior Pastor of the Pentecostal Church of Christ and President and Chair of the Joint College of African American Pentecostal Bishops, whose faith in me and encouragement during my ordination have had a lasting effect on my years as a pastor. His friendship and fellowship mean more than words can say, and my heart is grateful to him today.

This labor of love I dedicate to these five—my own personal heroes of faith.

TABLE OF CONTENTS

FOREWORD

"The Dr. Emma L. Creamer is one of the remaining LEGENDS of the Gospel Ministry, from a classy and feminine perspective. Her regal ability to reach and reward the Kingdom, all across the country has served as a lucid light in dark times. I grew up listening to her as a child as she trailblazed paths of preaching that today, MANY sisters trod. ANYTHING she reveals in this book must be received as Precious Nuggets."

Reverend Larry Phillip McCray
Mount Calvary Missionary Baptist Church
Temple Hills, Maryland

"Pastor Creamer has blessed our city and me through her walk of faith and her ability to overcome opposition and reign as "More Than A Conqueror." Her life's story will inspire you to heed the calling of God on your life and to never give up."

Apostle Thomas Wesley Weeks, Sr.
New Destiny Fellowship
Wilmington, Delaware

"I have known Pastor Creamer since she was 17 years old. I am aware of much she had to overcome to reach this point. She was faithful as a musician for her church. She was faithful in singing to the glory of God. God saw her faithfulness and elevated her to an evangelist and then to the pastorate. She is an example for any young woman who desires to give

her life in the service of the Lord and I am proud of her. LOOK WHAT THE LORD HAS DONE!!!!!!"

Audrey F. Bronson, Pastor
Sanctuary Church of the Open Door
Philadelphia, PA
Presiding Prelate of International
Fellowship of Churches

"I met Pastor Emma Creamer shortly after she relocated from Pennsylvania to Wilmington, Delaware. We were very young, only a few years removed from high school. We were very active in dynamic local ministries and being mentored by leaders who nurtured us in Christ. Pastor Creamer's musical gifts impacted her church and eventually brought her to the attention of gospel artists nationally. However, music was merely a step on her journey. God had a greater plan. The best was yet to come. Our friendship endures until this day in spite of challenges in our lives that continue to test our faith. At the end of each test, there is a testimony. Thank God for victory. Pastor Creamer, your journey of faithfulness and obedience has led you to great success in the gospel ministry. Today, the Cathedral of Fresh Fire you founded in Wilmington, Delaware is a thriving ministry under your dynamic leadership. I am honored to be your friend. Your inspirational journey described in this wonderful memoir is a blessing to the body of Christ. Continue to impact the world with your gifts and anointing as you journey to becoming all God has called you to be."

Reverend Garnita M. Selby, Esquire
Holy Temple Church of the Fresh Harvest
Penns Grove, New Jersey

PREFACE

A paradox of life is that often the circumstances and events that lead to greatness take place in the hidden years when few are looking and no one cares. This is a journey past sorrow to joy, and a trek from tragedy to triumph. On an unforgettable September day, God sent to the earth a very special kind of gift.

We know, of course, that nothing's as precious as Jesus, and God loved this world so much that He gave His only begotten Son so that whoever believes in Him will not perish but will have everlasting life. The phenomenal Christ, the King of all kings, is without doubt most assuredly unparalleled and forever without an equal. Jesus is God' greatest and most insurmountable gift to humankind. Christ is the Son of the living God. He has no equal. He has no peers. He is immutable, immortal, and invincible. God is God all by Himself – able to do what He wants, when He wants, how He wants. He is the giver of every good and perfect gift. So the day Emma Curry was born, God gave the 21st century body of Christ a girl who would impact this nation on His behalf. Her name is Emma, a name that derives from Emmanuel meaning "God is with us."

I met Pastor Creamer when I moved from Pennsylvania to Delaware in 1993. My life was at a turning point when I arrived in Delaware, and I was in desperate need of God's help, His guidance, and His healing. I'd been a Christian for about ten years when I came to Delaware, and I immediately began looking for a new church. One day I looked through the telephone book for churches to attend, and a phone referral led me to the church where Pastor Emma Creamer was ministering. The first time I attended her church, the sun was streaming in brightly through the floor-to-ceiling windows. Pastor Creamer and her praise team wore white dresses and beanies, and I was overwhelmed by the way they sang and praised and worshipped God. For the first time in a long time, I had been able to relax and worship God in my own way. It was exactly what my soul needed, and I left there feeling refreshed, restored, and renewed.

I visited other churches, but there was something about the praises at Pastor Creamer's church that drew me back. They gave God His ultimate praises and His due glory every single week without fail. I joined the church in 1994 and soon became interested in becoming a part of the ministry. I was so impressed with the level of excellence with which they conducted one of the annual baptism services, that I remember telling Deaconess Carolyn Martin that I wanted to wear a beanie too. In 1995, I became ordained as a deacon and began what has been my own incredible journey in Pastor Creamer's ministry.

After a morning service in late 1996, I felt led to tell Pastor Creamer that God was going to free me to be able to help her build her new ministry. A week later, I lost my husband of 24 years, the late William Harris Way, to sudden heart failure. It was late at night, but Pastor Creamer and Deaconess Martin drove me to the hospital to identify his body on the night that he died. I was devastated, stunned, numb. I had become a young widow without warning, but Pastor and her ministry were there for me at the lowest point of my life. I will always be grateful for that. She provided a place for me in her ministry, and I became busy helping her build the new ministry. It lessened my pain as a young widow, and I was healing gradually in the service of the Lord. As Ruth was to Naomi, so I was to Pastor Creamer. Wherever she went, I went; her people were my people; and her God was my God. Just like God blessed Ruth with Boaz, God blessed me with my own type of Boaz – my husband, Marshall Thomas Washington, who I met in her church after ten years of widowhood. This is proof that if you serve God faithfully, He will bless you "above measure." I have been blessed to serve by her side in various capacities from deacon and adjutant to administrative assistant and elder. Her powerful ministry has benefited my life in so many ways, and I am honored to be able to present her incredible life story to you.

These memoirs are quite unique in that they are written from a three-way perspective. First, there are times when Pastor Creamer's exact words are quoted. At other times, I have reported the events of her life as she has described them to me. Thirdly, I have included many of my own personal, firsthand experiences as a member of her ministry for the past 19 years. In addition, the life lessons at the end of the chapters and the principles presented throughout are included to provide the finishing complement of inspiration, encouragement, and faith that we hope you will gain from Pastor's journey of faith. During her rich and rewarding life's journey, she has been variously referred to as Emma, Emma Curry, Emma Loretta Curry Creamer, Emma Creamer, Evangelist Creamer, Pastor, and Pastor Creamer.

The story of Emma Loretta Curry Creamer chronicles

the strength of the human spirit when helped by the Spirit of God. This is a life on an intriguing path of twists and sudden turns, dangerous curves and fearsome forks in an often dark and sometimes lonely road. Let your heart be lifted as you experience in these pages the obstacles she overcame, the attacks she withstood, the enemies she defeated, and the victories she enjoyed. Join us in this journey of faith and learn what it takes to win over impossible odds and circumstances stacked so high that they cast a dark shadow over your future and seem at times to obscure your faith.

Gain new hope and determination from a woman's story that is as stately in life's triumphs as she is statuesque physically, standing an even six feet tall. Just as faithful Abraham couldn't see the provision of God until he was near the top of Mount Moriah, likewise in the mountainside in upstate Pennsylvania we see the beginnings of Emma's arduous and awe-inspiring journey the entire distance from a broken piano to a pastor's pulpit.

The story of Emma Creamer is presented with a focus on the faithfulness of God who is her Savior, Deliverer, Healer, Provider, and Keeper. You will find that the recurring theme of her life story always points up to God who is Omnipotent, Eternal, all good, and only good. Christ Jesus, the Son of God and Savior of mankind is the highlight of this work, and the precious Holy Spirit, the eternal paracletos, has provided the strength and fortitude to complete this book. Take the time to treasure God's presence between each line of this story.

As you read, rise above the visible text and see for yourself the provision of God, the protection of God, and the promotion of God. Focus your mind on the intent of this work: to glorify God, to magnify Jesus Christ, to exalt the Holy Spirit, and to praise the God of our salvation. None can claim equality with His majesty, His highness, or His holiness. We merely attempt to illustrate herein that if we will trust God in obedience and childlike faith, He Himself will uphold, preserve, and sustain us forever. This is about the splendor of surrender to the sovereign will of God and the treasure of turning oneself over completely to Him. Enjoy the journey, and as you read, reflect on the truth that nothing's as precious as Jesus, my friend, nothing's as precious as He.

ACKNOWLEDGEMENTS

This page is to express my overwhelming gratitude to every one who God sent to walk with me at one point or another on my journey of faith. My life story could not have been written without you.

In memoriam, I will forever be grateful for those whom I've loved and known who have gone on to be with the Lord. My mother, Olive Curry, Elder Rainey, Jim, Calvin, June, Virginia, Dr. Howard, Mom Phoebe, the church mothers, and so many other generals of the faith who impacted my life more than words can say. I thank God with all of my heart that I had each of you in my life.

My heart overflows with gratitude to God for all of my natural family, especially Alleen, Twyla, Yarah, Andre, Helena, Chuck, Milana, Malcolm, Marcus, Nasia, and Neiko. There aren't words to describe how you have enriched my life. I love you all — you are my pride and joy.

Also, I will always be grateful for each and every one of my Cathedral family ministry, members, friends, and supporters. I wouldn't trade you for the world – you are the best people God could have ever blessed me with. I thank you once, I thank you twice, I thank you over and over again.

How can I say thanks for all the things God has done for me, and how can I thank the countless people He brought into my life to bless me as you all have done. I will always be grateful for your love, your support, your prayers, your giving, and your friendship. Each of you is an integral part of my life and my life story, and I could not have done what I've done without you.

If I had ten thousand tongues with which to praise Him, I could not enough my blessed Lord adore for all that you each mean to me. My life is rich and complete because of you. May God bless you exceeding abundantly above all that you can ask or imagine. My love, my thanks, and my prayers always –

Your Pastor, Mother, Sister, Friend,

Emma L. Creamer

CHAPTER 1

CHOSEN

✝

The late Mother Olive Curry of Altoona, PA said this to her daughter, Emma, the middle child of her seven children, who sometimes wore Mother Olive's own shoes to church: *"God has chosen you."*

"Ye have not chosen me, but I have chosen you, and ordained you that ye should go and bring forth fruit, and that your fruit should remain: that whatsoever ye shall ask of the Father in my name, he may give it you."
John 15:16

Childhood Memories

"Well, let's see," says the now wise and seasoned Pastor Emma Creamer as she contemplates her humble beginnings. "I was born on September 6th in a little town called Hollidaysburg in Pennsylvania, and I know that God had purpose for my life even before I was in my mother's womb. God purposed all these things that I have been through, and I appreciate Him. I appreciate Him. When I think as far back as I can, I remember that my mother had seven children, and I was the middle child of the seven. I had two sisters, June and Alleen, and a brother, Calvin who were older than me, and a brother, Jim, and two sisters, Virginia and Twyla, who were younger than me. At that time, I certainly did not know what was going on in my life, but God had purpose."

Pastor Creamer continues: "God has purpose for each of us. I was raised in the church. I got saved when I was around seven or eight years old. From Hollidaysburg we moved to Altoona, Pennsylvania, and that's where God connected my mother with one of the church mothers, Mother Daisy Moore. The two of them were very instrumental in my life, and that's how I became the woman I am. I didn't always want to hear what they had to say, but somehow when God has His hands on you, you can't get away. You just can't. God put a spirit of obedience in me so that I would be obedient and hear what they had to say."

"I started playing the piano when I was right around seven years old. And before I even played in church, I remember the piano that we had in our home was a somewhat old piano. The spirit of the Lord must have been in that piano because I started playing and had never taken a lesson – not a single lesson. The first song I remember playing was "Jesus Loves Me." Truly, after all these years have passed by, I can truly say that He has and He does love me. I remember playing and trying to sing a little bit."

"My mother and father separated when I was very young. After going through a few periods of trouble at a young age and living with my grandmother, we ended up moving into Altoona. There we lived above the church that we attended. I believe the name of the church was Gethsemane Church of God in Christ. We lived right up above the church. I ended up playing the piano there in the church. I didn't really know how to play the piano, but I played. I remember the old songs that they sang like "I'm a Soldier in the Army of the Lord" and all those other old songs. Don't ask me how it sounded when I was playing – I was just playing. I was obeying my mom and the church mother, Mother Moore."

"I remember being a young girl at seven or eight years old belonging to a team called the Booker T. Washington Softball Team. By the time I was eight or nine, Mother Moore had children. One of her children was named Regina Moore, and we had a little team we played on together. I remember very distinctly that I was supposed to go play softball one Sunday when we were having an afternoon service at church. The services started at three o'clock in the afternoon. During that time, we would go to church in the morning, and we wouldn't leave until that evening. Even though we lived upstairs, we didn't go upstairs. We just stayed in the church all day."

"The three o'clock service was scheduled, but I wanted to go play softball. I remember that my mother and Mother Moore wouldn't let me go. I didn't understand why I couldn't go even though Regina was going. So I asked why I couldn't go because

Regina was going, and Mother Moore said to me, 'Because there is a calling on your life.' I didn't understand what she meant when she said I had 'a calling on my life.' My mother was a very strong disciplinarian, and we had to be obedient. If we weren't obedient, she took care of business. So I stayed for that service, and I guess that was the beginning of God actually speaking to me so I could understand what He was trying to say. It was difficult at that time, though, because I was just a child."

"Mother Moore knew of the calling on my life because of her own relationship with God and the presence of the Holy Spirit in her life. She was able to recognize the message God was giving her about me. And since I was a child and not yet able to understand God or the Holy Spirit, God made the information available to me through Mother Moore—someone more mature in her relationship with God and knowledgeable about how He works in our lives through His word, His Son, His Spirit, and His people."

"Not enough can be said of the blessing and benefit it is to have one of the old church mothers in your life. They are invaluable and priceless blessings. We all need their wise counsel and guidance, and I thank my God for the mothers of the church who help the younger saints make it through this narrow way."

The beauty of having God's hand on your life at such an early age is remarkable. What troubles, problems, difficulties, and pain could be averted and avoided if people would turn to God while they are young. How much more blessed and how much less burdened their lives would be. Perhaps teenage promiscuity and teen pregnancy would be less prevalent if young people would listen, trust God, and obey. Perhaps there would be less drug and alcohol use among the young. Maybe there'd be a lower suicide rate among teenagers or fewer school dropouts. It is reasonable to presume that a young person's life would probably follow a course that is destined for more success if he or she chose Christ sooner in life rather than later. "God blessed me with sooner," Emma recalls, "and credit for God's call on my life is not mine, of course. God decided He'd choose me. It was His alone to decide."

Christ yielded to the will of the Father in the Garden of Gethsemane. Young Emma also had "nevertheless" moments of her own at the start of her journey of faith. Christ's "nevertheless" transitioned Him to His seat at the right hand of God, the Father. Christ's surrender to His painful path to glory qualified Him for His present position of exaltation above every name that is named. Christ's "nevertheless" was a precursor to the "nevertheless" every Christian must eventually embrace if he or she is to transition to a place of power and glory in this life or the next.

Emma Curry at age 19

Young Emma did not know then that she would live the "nevertheless" many times over the course of her journey. Nevertheless, she played the piano in church while the other children played outside. Nevertheless, she learned to be obedient while still young. No, she did not always want to be obedient, to submit, or to yield to the will of God and the call on her life. But this was God's call, not hers. Her life is God's life. Thankfully she came to realize that fact while she was very young, and that knowledge has sustained her faith throughout the trying, troublesome, and difficult times of her life. Her answer was "yes," and she meant it with her whole heart. God had won her heart at the tender age of nine. She was His and He was hers, and that was God's plan for her life.

A General of the Faith

Emma's mother was strict and stern, yet extremely faithful to God. She made all her children, especially Emma, obey all the church elders. She kept them in church and encouraged them. Wherever her mother went, Emma went. Her mother had become a single parent with seven children. From a young age, her mother told her she was the chosen of God, but Emma didn't understand it then as a young child. Mother Curry was so determined to keep her children in church that Emma recalls having to wear her mother's shoes to service because she did not have her own.

Mother Curry was a disciplinarian, yet she was a loving and kind Christian woman who always had young people around her. She was very strong physically and did many things around the house. Emma was about nine years old when her natural father left them. They were very rich spiritually, though they did not have much materially back then. But Mother Curry, being the woman of great faith that she was, knew that God could do anything. She knew that God would take care of them all, and He always did. Sometimes if there was nothing for them to eat, Mother Curry would set the table anyway, knowing that they had no food that day. She carefully placed the clean plates and glasses, the knives, the forks, the napkins just where they belonged on her table. The cupboard was empty, but on their table was a place setting for each one of her children and herself. In faith, she did it. In faith, she believed God. God always honors that kind of faith and sure enough before the end of the day, there'd be a knock on the door, and someone would come with food for them all! That's the kind of woman Olive Curry was, and all of her children inherited this unusual kind of faith. She lived for God and did His will even when it was the most difficult thing for her to do. Mother Olive Curry would do anything for God. She loved God and lived for Him and taught all of her children how to live for Him too.

This is a remarkable story not only because of the remarkable faith that Emma inherited from her mother but also because of her remarkable obedience that ushered her into the ranks of the chosen few. Her surrender to her mother's mandates set her girlish feet onto a pathway of righteousness. Therein lies the power; therein is the key. The secret to being chosen may simply be one's propensity for obedience. Obedience to parents first, then to church mothers and elders and leaders, all of which really translates to obedience to God. Obedience is one of God's requisite ingredients in the human heart. Matthew Henry comments regarding Deuteronomy 28:1-14 that God prefers that we obey and live rather than sin and die, for the kind of obedience that "pleases best comes from a principle of delight in God's goodness." Young Emma's heart seemed turned toward the things of God well before she knew that she was God's chosen.

To be chosen is truly a position of privilege but its price tag is hidden like that of a very expensive item of jewelry in an exclusive display case. God chose Joseph and David for the leadership of His people. God's purpose is what distinguishes us, defines us, and differentiates us all. In Romans 8, Paul reminds us that whom God did foreknow, He also did predestinate. God makes purposeful choices that align with His future goals. His plan is to help people find Him. God knows who to designate for these divine assignments. His choices always fare well in the retrospective view. From Noah to Abraham, from Joseph to Moses, from Joshua to Samuel, and from David to Jesus, the ranks of those chosen speak of God's amazing ability to place within a person the exact quality that He intends to extract from them to further His cause. God knows what is inside of a man, and God knows how much He can get out of that man. He knows how much of what God needs the man will yield to Him because God is omniscient.

If many are called but few chosen as the Bible says, then to what exactly have they been called and chosen to do? They are called to exchange their sin for Christ's righteousness. They are called to become clothed in His righteousness. The call is first to salvation through Christ. They are chosen to become able and productive ambassadors for Christ. They've been called to promote and spread His gospel of good news in their own proverbial Jerusalems, Judeas, Samarias, and uttermost parts of the earth. They have been chosen to carry forward the message of God through His Son Jesus in the way He has designed for their lives. They have not been chosen as a select group who just happen to be part of an exclusive society of the elect or elite. No, they are chosen because of their aptitude for obedience to God's call on them.

They actually go where God leads and say what God says. The few chosen are special and unique only in their actions of obedience founded on their faith in Him. Those chosen have this in common: they've embraced Christ as their worthy Ruler who knows better than they and therefore warrants their absolute obedience and unwavering trust. A chosen vessel is a willing vessel who accomplishes the Master's goals and performs the Master's will. The old people used to sing, "The Lord has laid His hand on me!" How marvelous to be arrested and detained by God's purpose and to find oneself positioned ever so graciously among God's chosen few. God knows where we should be and when we should be there. God knew how to position Emma for greatness and exactly where He wanted her to be. God knew, so He brought Elder Ross B. Rainey into her life.

A Man After God's Own Heart

Ross B. Rainey was sent to Altoona from Philadelphia by Bishop Ozra Thurston Jones, Sr., one of the five original bishops of the Church of God in Christ International. Rainey was ordained a minister under Bishop O.T. Jones, Sr., and he & O.T. Jones, Jr. were like brothers. While he was in Altoona, Rev. Rainey met Olive Curry. Emma was eight or nine years old at that time. Mother Curry was saved under Rev. Rainey, so she had a great deal of respect for him as a man of God. Through the years, they referred to him either as Reverend Rainey or Elder Rainey.

Elder Rainey met and fell in love with Mother Daisy Moore's daughter, Thelma, and they were married. Not long after that, Bishop O.T. Jones. Sr., sent Elder Rainey and his wife, Thelma, to Delaware to build the first Church of God in Christ there. Elder Rainey had seen young Emma playing the piano at Gethsemane Church of God in Christ in Altoona before he and Sister Rainey left for Delaware. But because he was truly a visionary, Elder Rainey saw more than just a young girl playing the piano. God had placed His Spirit in Rev. Rainey and given Emma favor with him. He seemed to already know in his heart that young Emma was God's chosen one.

As they were building their new church in Delaware, Elder Rainey came to Miss Olive with a question one day that would change the course of young Emma's life. He asked if she would allow Emma to come and play the piano at their new church in Delaware. But, Emma was only 14 at the time, and Delaware was more than 200 miles from Altoona. Emma did not want to leave her home or her family at the tender of age 14. She loved her mother and her brothers and sisters very much and had no desire to be away from them in an unfamiliar place.

The Curry Family with Dad (William) and Mom (Olive) Watching Over (l to r) June, Alleen, Emma, Jim, Virginia, Twyla and Calvin (seated)

Seven is God's Perfect Number

Her three older siblings are June, Alleen, and Calvin. She, Emma, was in the middle, and her three younger siblings are Jim, Virginia, and Twyla. They all went to church together and gave their lives to the Lord as young people mainly because of their mother's influence on their lives. Miss Olive's love of God impacted them all greatly, and though Emma left home at age 14, she remembers that all of her siblings loved God and each one of them ultimately lived their lives in service to Him in their own unique ways.

Today, she recalls her deceased siblings: June, Calvin, Jim, and Virginia. Calvin, their oldest brother was a quite strong man who was not afraid of hard work. He had come to know the Lord and went home peacefully to his eternal rest. June was a special lady with an endearing smile who had been a missionary before she died. Virginia, strong and tall, had loved and served the Lord as a minister before her passing. Jim was also a very spiritual person who had enjoyed a successful career playing professional football for the Dallas Cowboys. They were strong people who had loved and served the Lord. Most of them remained in the Altoona area, except for Virginia who ministered in North Carolina for many years.

Emma also cherishes her two living sisters today – Alleen and Twyla. Her sister, Alleen, joined with her and has been helping her in ministry for many years. Alleen loves God and His word, and she is a currently a member of the Mother's Board of the Cathedral of Fresh Fire in Wilmington. Twyla, who is the youngest daughter, is a stately woman with a commanding presence and engaging smile. Twyla is an ordained elder who lives and ministers in North Carolina. Each one of Miss Olive's children was influenced deeply by her great love of God, and each of them became God's servants in their own unique way.

When the Cloud of Glory is Moving, Move With the Cloud

Mother Curry had no prior thought or intent to allow her middle child to leave her at such a young age. But Olive Curry had become saved under Reverend Rainey, so she had a great deal of respect for him and knew that his ministry was genuine and effective. Therefore, when Rev. Rainey asked if Emma could come to help him in his ministry, how could she deny his request? Human thinking falls far short of the ideas of the Creator who is not only able to do far more than we can even imagine, but actually carries out His powerful will routinely and inevitably. No one who God chooses escapes the sovereign and directive guidance of God, the Holy Spirit, because only God has the divine power and omniscience to make things happen to and for us that we cannot make happen for ourselves. He also protects as He directs, so the safest place to be is in the perfect will of God.

Mother Curry loved God. She would do anything to please Him. So courageously and faithfully, she consented to allow Emma to go to Delaware to live with Elder Ross Rainey and his wife, the late Sister Thelma Rainey. Mother Curry did it because she loved God and had unwavering faith in Him. She believed Emma would be fine under Reverend and Sister Rainey's care. Perhaps Mother Olive even hoped that Emma might even have a better life in this new place.

At first, Emma did not really want to leave her home and

her family, but eventually God put it in her spirit and off she went on the 200+ mile journey from Altoona, Pennsylvania to the town of Wilmington in Delaware. Emma was only 14 years old when she left home. The Raineys took her in and cared for her like their very own daughter. Rev. Rainey became Emma's spiritual father, training her in the way she should go, teaching her the elements of the faith, and giving her the opportunity to grow into a great spiritual leader. She was graciously received not only by Elder Rainey but also by his wife, the late Mother Thelma Rainey. Mother Rainey helped take care of Emma like she was her very own. She stood with her husband, Elder Rainey, in continuing the work begun by Emma's natural mother. For the teenage Emma, Mother Rainey became one of the priceless people who pour into a young person's life and help to make them what God has designed. She became Emma's mother away from home. Together, Elder and Mother Rainey were instrumental in Emma's development into an evangelist, pastor, and eventual leader of a major ministry.

Her obedience uncovered the truth that the faithful and precious leading of the Holy Spirit of God will never fail to manifest a great harvest in the lives of the obedient – a huge harvest of righteousness, peace, and joy in the Holy Ghost. No lives can we impact with such great change as when we go where God leads, trusting that at the end of that road, we will find blessing, and benefit, and peace.

Faith and Obedience Are Relatives

The crucial and critical principle that Emma learned is obedience. She, just like the Jesus who saved her so young, would learn obedience from the things that she suffered. Young Emma may not have understood as a child that obedience is better than sacrifice. But thank God that He not only gave her the gift of faith, but He gave her the gift of obedience too.

Obedience is better than going our own way. Obedience ever triumphs over its antithesis. And if we suffer for our obedience, then we have a promise that we will reign with the one who suffered for us: the man Christ Jesus. Obedience is a recurring theme throughout her tenure later as a leader among leaders. It's the kind of obedience that caused her to be able to leave her family and the comfort of her home town and begin to minister in a strange land among unfamiliar surroundings. It's the kind of obedience that refuses to compromise with the forces of darkness. Obedience takes a great deal of faith, too. In fact, it is mostly faith that constitutes obedience and without faith it is not only impossible to please God, but it is also impossible to maintain obedience. Faith is the foundational truth and the durable platform on which her success has been built.

Obedience to God is a paramount theme and an obvious requisite to the calling of God to His holy work. Together with faith, obedience helps us to live above feelings and circumstances and the opinions of man. How powerful it is to yield your power to God's so His power can transform you and a multitude following you. Emma was chosen to believe and obey, and that is exactly what she did. Years later when she'd been in ministry many years, Emma's close friend, the late Dr. L. Ramona Howard told her that God would always bless her because she had a "spirit of obedience."

We are challenged by this to take the same kind of steps of faith in our own personal journeys. Emma's example provides a powerful illustration for our own lives. If you are a young person reading this, will you yield to the authority figures in your own life? Will you humble yourself as young Emma did as she played the piano in church instead of going out to have fun with the other children? Is your heart tender toward God and His ways? Are you willing to do what you are told in spite of how you may feel? Let's simply choose to obey God in all of our circumstances. We, too, are called to obey and chosen to believe. We'll see in the pages ahead the blessings and the benefits that God poured on this precious life. Because she both trusted and obeyed is perhaps what caused Emma Creamer to be both called and chosen.

LIFE LESSON 1
All God Wants Is A "Yes!"

A man who was once called to preach decided that he would not obey God's calling on his life. He tried to run away from that calling and chose a life of alcoholism instead. The man became known for sitting on a street curb, and though usually drunk, he preached to the passersby on the street instead of preaching from a church pulpit (which was God's original choice and intention for his life).

God's choice is sometimes not ours, but God's choice is always the best choice. If an individual is chosen by God for a specific assignment, God never changes His mind, and that person will eventually fulfill the designated assignment. When God calls, the only correct answer is "Yes, Lord." In this way, we avoid sinking our lives into the gutter of regrets, and God Himself becomes the glory and the lifter of our heads and our lives.

How can two walk together unless they agree? We do well to agree with the God who created us. This agreement will involve surrender to His sovereign will, for He will not compromise with human willfulness. God is not a people-pleaser—He is a people-lifter and a people-lover. He is the Creator and Sovereign Ruler over all, and wisdom says agree quickly with Him. We can enjoy a life without regret when our answer to God is "Yes."

CHAPTER 2

RISE ABOVE THE VISIBLE

✝

Reverend Rainey loved to preach and wanted to build a cathedral for God. Pastor Creamer eventually built that cathedral and dedicated the Ross B. Rainey Fellowship Hall to him in memoriam for the great impact that Reverend Rainey had on her life and her ministry. Her life was changed by his teaching: *"Rise above the visible and see God."*

"For we walk by faith, not by sight."
II Corinthians 5:7

The Late Reverend Ross B. Rainey
"Rise above the visible and see God."

God began unfolding His masterful plan for Emma's life early on by placing Rev. Rainey in her life. Pastor Creamer fondly recalls Reverend Ross B. Rainey's influence on her life. "Many of the lessons I learned, I learned from Rev. Rainey and Mother Curry." "I lived with the Rainey family and worked in the church." He was a very powerful, strong, God-fearing, loving man. Elder Rainey loved God and loved God's people. He was quite an example for God's people. He loved to preach about God, and the power, sovereignty, omnipotence, and omnipresence of God. Elder Rainey was a thin and somewhat soft-spoken man but he became known for his powerful saying, 'Rise above the visible and see God.'"

Emma says that Rev. Rainey was inspired by God when he taught people how to depend on and have faith in God rather than on their circumstances and what they could see in the natural realm. As Emma made her way toward leadership in ministry, she tried to do just what Rev. Rainey had said: she tried to rise above what is seen in the natural realm and envision what God was doing in the spiritual realm. God was definitely using Rev. Rainey and others to let Emma know that she was being called up higher. Preparing to lead by learning to follow, her poignant pathway had been laid out by God. God always provides signals and signposts to guide and encourage us along our way toward destiny. He did that for Emma one night in a vivid dream.

The Dream

One night, Emma had a dream in which she vividly remembers seeing people running over to a fence. The fence was very high, and the people were jumping up in an attempt to see over it. In the dream, Emma heard a voice tell her clearly, "If you stand on your tiptoes, you're tall enough." She stood up on her tiptoes and saw a green pasture that was beautiful, lush, and peaceful, where God's Spirit was moving back and forth ever so gracefully. In her heart, she knew exactly what God meant by this dream. He was showing her that He had already given her exactly what she needed to be able to rise above the visible. The fence probably represented some of the obstacles and blockages she would encounter along the way. However, the blockages could never stop or hinder her if she would utilize the gifts with which she had already been blessed.

God was showing her that she could obtain this place where His Spirit controls everything and causes it to be peaceful, graceful, flourishing, and full. He showed her a place that resembled the very character of Christ that is full of grace and truth. This is the place where God wants us to go, and He encourages us to rise above what is immediately in front of us in the natural realm and to look past those things that would deter us and distract us. God wants us to look toward those places where His Spirit brings peace and tranquility, order and rest. It is essential for us to look in the direction that God is pointing us toward and to fix our focus on His goal, His plan, and His purpose for our lives. God wants us to look past the walls of worrisome problems and the fences that block our blessings. He was sharpening Emma's spiritual vision so she could journey on in trust, in hope, and in faith.

We, too, are tall enough to be able to see past what blocks our view of God and His will for our lives. Stretch yourself beyond your comfort zone and refuse to allow walls and fences to stand in your way. This is what Emma did. She stretched herself beyond her own ideas and thoughts. She reached past her own will and emotions. She used faith in God and the integrity of His word to stretch her faith up toward what human eyes cannot see. Abraham could not see the ram in the bush until he had gone all the way up to the top of Mount Moriah. So we should rise above where we are and get up to a place with a wider perspective of the world that God has in store for us. That is where the provision for our miracle awaits, and God leads us to the place of our miracles step by faithful and obedient step. Abraham carried Isaac to the top of Mount Moriah, step by faithful and obedient step. It was there that he heard God's voice and saw God's provision.

So rise above is what Emma proceeded to do. She continued to help Elder Rainey and worked faithfully in the church. Emma was taking her own steps of obedience and faith, and just like faithful Abraham, she was about to hear God's voice, too.

When God Calls

It came on a night way back in 1973. Emma received an urgent call. It turned out to be the most important call of her life. She was at home in Wilmington — in the right place at the right time. God's perfect timing sometimes catches us off guard. It came unexpectedly like a sudden downpour does on a sunny summer day. Suddenly, almost out of nowhere, the call came.

She's not sure if it was very late at night, or maybe it was in the wee, small hours of the morning. She also couldn't tell if she was dreaming or not. All Emma knows is that she heard God's still, small voice clearly and distinctly down deep in her heart. God spoke these profoundly life-changing words: *"I have called you to preach."*

God was calling her to preach? Yes! God was calling _her_, Emma, to preach! God chose her and now He had called her. His call had come without any warning just like a thief in the night! The call to preach – the most important call anyone could ever get – had come suddenly. She was astounded, excited, and shocked all at the same time and could hardly sleep for the rest of that night. When morning finally arrived after what seemed like the longest night of her life, Emma jumped up and hurriedly readied herself to leave the house. It seemed like she could net get ready fast enough. Finally, Emma threw open her front door and broke out into a run down the Wilmington street. With her mind racing faster than her feet could take her, Emma ran all 20 of the blocks that separated her house from the church. Reverend Rainey was working in the church just as he always did. Emma knew he'd be there. Out-of-breath and overwhelmed with excitement and joy and fear, Emma blurted out these words to her spiritual dad: "Elder Rainey, God has called me to preach!" The response he gave surprised her almost as much as what she'd heard the night before. Rainey looked at her with a slight smile and knowing eyes and replied in a very matter-of-fact tone, "I know it – I just wanted you to know it!" He knew it like pastors of soon-to-be-pastors usually do. He did not try to hide the fact that it was no surprise to him. God had already spoken to him to "put Emma in preparation," and he knew what that meant. Now, God was simply executing His holy and sovereign plan. Rev. Rainey knew that, and now Emma did, too. A short time later, Rev. Rainey scheduled her first sermon for a Sunday evening service at the church. The initial (or trial) sermon is an important rite of passage for a preacher, so at age 34, Emma began her preaching career with her first message entitled, We Need A Reminder.

Initially, she became a missionary and doors began to open throughout the U.S. and abroad. Creamer was called on to minister at A.M.E., Baptist, and Pentecostal churches alike. Her powerfully anointed voice would invariably move the congregations to shouts of joy and praise, and her services were exhilarating, uplifting, and life changing. She was gifted to sing and had now been called to preach, but back then, she much preferred ministering in song. It would be some years later that she would fully accept her call to the preaching ministry. Her gifts continued to make room for her, though, both here and abroad.

Evangelist Emma Creamer in the Holy Land in Israel

God, the Rewarder

Evangelist Creamer was receiving regular invitations to minister during that time. On one occasion, Reverend Morgan Powell invited her to deliver the keynote speech at a Bible school graduation in Coatesville, Pennsylvania—a small town outside of Philadelphia. She accepted the invitation and spoke at the graduation. God gave her tremendous favor, and a few days after the graduation, Rev. Powell called Evangelist Creamer and offered her an unusual and unexpected speaker's "honorarium." Rev. Powell's church gave her a 10-day, expense-paid trip for two to the Holy Land in Israel! God rewards, and He uses people to do it for Him! God is a rewarder of those who diligently seek Him

(Hebrews 11:6), and every good and perfect gift is from above and cometh down from the Father of lights (James 1:17). So Evangelist Creamer and Dr. Howard took off for the Holy Land of Israel. Their plane landed in Jordan after a 22-hour flight. Evangelist Creamer was blessed to minister in song all throughout the Holy Land including a baptism at the Jordan River – the place where our dear Lord Jesus Himself was baptized. What a glorious, exhilarating, and unusually anointed time it was — a trip of a lifetime that did not cost her a dime. The lyrics to this song that she sang while riding a tour bus in Israel illustrate how highly blessed she felt:

> ♫ *Something in my heart like a stream running down,*
> *Makes me feel so happy, happy as can be.*
> *When I think of Jesus and what He's done for me,*
> *Something in my heart like a stream running down.*

Surrounded by Greatness

Evangelist Creamer continued to rise above the visible, and her gifts became the vehicle in which she rode. She was living Proverbs 18:16: *"A man's gift maketh room for him, and bringeth him before great men."* Her gifts were making room for her and bringing her before great women, too! God blessed her with the opportunity to sing with Dorothy Norwood, one of the greatest gospel singers of all time. Norwood is affectionately known as the "greatest storyteller of all time," and Evangelist Creamer really enjoyed the time she spent singing with the Grammy and Stellar Award nominee. Creamer also sang with Shirley Caesar, the Roger Roberts Singers, and the Cloud Davis Specials. God has given every good and perfect gift and for those who will agree to use those gifts in His honor and for His glory, God lifts us up and positions and us in ever-higher places in Him. Evangelist Creamer's gifts made room for her in the places she visited including the Holy Land and the island of Bermuda. Her music ministry was very successful. She formed her own group known as the Emma Creamer Singers with the late Dr. L. Ramona Howard, Elder Delnora Roberts, and Elder Tammy Lindsay. They recorded three successful albums: <u>Call on Jesus</u>, <u>There's Nothing As Precious As Jesus</u>, and <u>Move With the Spirit</u>. This statuesque lady with the hazel eyes and anointed voice was enjoying the favor and blessings of God in her preaching ministry, her music ministry, and her personal life as well.

Marriage Is Honorable

Emma met, fell in love with, and married a handsome and charming young man named Leon Creamer. God had not only gifted her with the ability to play music by ear and an anointed singing voice, but He was about to bless her even more with three beautiful children. Yarah is the firstborn daughter of Leon and Emma Creamer. An honest and forthright personality, Yarah is a statuesque woman who loves the Lord Jesus Christ and lives her life in service to Him along with her husband, Charles, and their three exceptional children: Milana, Malcolm, and Marcus. Yarah and her family are powerful witnesses for Christ who demonstrate uncompromising faith and unwavering commitment to the cause of Christ. About her mother, Yarah said, "We have seen you wait on the Lord as you displayed good courage – this has been one of the most valuable lessons you have taught us."

As God continued to elevate her, Evangelist Creamer had her second child, her son LeAndre. A charming, handsome, and athletic boy, Andre became an outstanding football player with a winning personality. His athletic skill earned him a full scholarship to the University of Tennessee at Knoxville, after which he began to enjoy a successful career coaching college football. Andre is a man of great charisma, and he and his beautiful wife, Tawanna, had two beautiful children: Nasia and Neiko. All five of Pastor Creamer's grandchildren are smart, beautiful, handsome, and blessed, and she is extremely proud of each one of them. Her son, Andre, describes his love and admiration for his mother in this way: "I have watched you for 42 years and **never** have you made me feel embarrassed to be your son. You have and continue to inspire me with your willingness to give God your best."

**Yarah Creamer Gilbert and Family (l to r)
Malcolm, Charles, Marcus, Yarah, Milana**

**LeAndre Creamer and Family
(l to r) Neiko, Tawanna (seated), Nasia,
Andre**

Evangelist Creamer became seriously ill during the time of her third pregnancy. The doctors advised her to terminate the pregnancy, but in her customary faith-filled fashion, she refused. She told the doctors that God had shown her the girl, with whom she was pregnant, playing under a table with her other children, Yarah and Andre. The doctor seemed surprised that she knew the unborn child was a girl. Her faith would again lift her up above what could be seen, and she eventually had her third child, a beautiful daughter whom she named Helena. Helena also had exceptional athletic ability and was a successful basketball player in high school. She earned a full scholarship to North Carolina A&T University, after which she, too, began a successful career coaching women's college basketball. But, Helena knew she had a calling from God on her life. At the age of 12, Helena told Evangelist Creamer that God wanted her to be a missionary. Elder Rainey's admonition to rise above the visible was a strong influence in Helena's life, too, and she eventually left her coaching career to work closely by her mother's side helping her to build God's ministry. Not long ago, Helena said these words about her mother: "You're a wonderful mother, so gentle, yet so strong . . . If I had my choice of mothers, trust me, you'd be the one I'd select."

Even with the responsibilities of motherhood, God continued to elevate Evangelist Creamer while she was raising her three children. When they were still young and she was a national evangelist traveling for the COGIC organization, she would bring Yarah, Andre, and Helena along whenever she went to sing, evangelize, and preach. Raising children is a huge challenge when the working mother has a normal job, but imagine traveling from city to city to preach bringing your three children everywhere that you go. She taught her children the great lessons of faith she had learned. They knew and loved Reverend Rainey too. They, too, were learning his lessons of faith. They were listening to their mother sing and pray and preach. They were hearing about God and learning about Christ. They were learning how to trust and obey. She was showing them by example that they could conquer any foe. From a broken piano to a pastor's pulpit, Evangelist Creamer was leading them and training them up in the way they should go. She knew that even when they're old, they won't depart from it.

A mother needs her children as much as the children need their mother. Children provide comfort and joy as well as strength and support. Their presence tends to calm a mother's spirit and soothe her weary soul. Regardless of the mother's vocation, her children are her greatest blessing from God. Being a preacher's kid has many challenges like having to share their parent with the whole world. Yarah, LeAndre, and Helena Creamer have done this most graciously, and their mother has always been godly proud of each one of them. *"Children are a heritage from the Lord, the fruit of the womb is a reward.* (Psalm 127:3, NKJV)

Co-Pastor Helena M. Creamer
"Let the Lord use you."

He's Preparing Me

Reverend Rainey continued to obey God's directive to put her in preparation by appointing Evangelist Creamer as administrative assistant. She then became responsible for handling and overseeing most aspects of the church's business. She learned so much about how to love people during those days. Rainey would often sit her down and talk with her for hours at a time and tell her how to handle the situations that would arise within the church. Sometimes she would lose patience, but Elder Rainey's even-tempered wisdom always helped her. He was a kind and peaceful man who did not lose his temper or raise his voice. She learned from him and respected his leadership and guidance, though she admits that she did not always understand or agree with his advice. Elder Rainey expected obedience from her, and she was determined to never let him down.

Evangelist Creamer's relationship with Rev. Rainey was divinely ordered by God. God understood exactly whom He should use as her mentor in the faith, and Rev. Rainey executed his office well. He knew that God had called Emma to preach, because God had already spoken to him. "God told me to put you in preparation," said Elder Rainey. How blessed she was to have people in her life who knew the voice of God and knew how to act on it in obedience.

During her tenure as Rev. Rainey's administrative assistant, Evangelist Creamer wrote a prayer of agreement that Rev. Rainey signed. They needed God's help with a building fund project, so they did what they do best: they prayed. Little did she know that the prayer she wrote that day on Rev. Rainey's behalf would turn out to be quite prophetic and that the fulfillment of that prayer/prophecy would come years later in a way she would never expect. Here is the prayer Evangelist Creamer wrote:

"Dear Lord Our Father and God,

We as a body of believers and as an effort to support our pastor in the name of Jesus to grant he and ourselves the kind of money we need to do a job that has been overdue. Knowing that you know all things, you know what we need even before I write the next word. We believe that you are going to grant our request for the money to build you a building and beautify the building we are in. The pastor has signed this by faith, and I am writing this in faith and the church is praying in faith. Please answer our petition for we understand that there is nothing too hard for you. We love and adore you." *(signed by Rev. Ross B. Rainey)*

Rev. Rainey signed it, and their agreement of prayer was settled in heaven. They both knew about the power of prayer and were quite familiar with how God hears and answers prayers. God had answered so many of their prayers in the past, and they also knew that prayers of agreement are especially powerful and effective. She and Rev. Rainey knew God's promise in Matthew 18:19 very well: *" . . . if two you shall agree on earth as touching anything that they shall ask, it shall be done for them of my Father which is in heaven."* Evangelist Creamer knew that Rev. Rainey wanted to build a cathedral for God, and she was committed to helping her spiritual father however she could. Rev. Rainey, the visionary, was mentoring a visionary who was rising above the visible and seeing more and more of God.

Elevation in any dimension does not come without resistance. Rising is contrary to the laws of the physical realm. It requires opposition and defiance of the laws that govern gravity, and it opposes what keeps us held firmly down. To rise above, demands more than mere mortal strength. It takes faith to pursue the unseen. We must set our determined sights high up. We must look above to what God has for us. Like Evangelist Creamer with her children along for the ride, we must buckle up, and prepare to do what the late Reverend Rainey admonished us to do. We must follow his powerful example. We must rise above what we see and past what we feel. We go higher than what looks scary and beyond all our fears. For if we can look up, we can get up, and if we can get up, we can rise up to where God's wonderful will is for us. How you ask do I rise from where I am? Well as Pastor Creamer has herself so eloquently said: "God won't put in a state of confusion. If you'll listen, He'll tell you exactly what to do." Just listen, my friend, God is speaking to you.

LIFE LESSON 2
"You Better See This Thing!"

What we experience in the physical realm is limited by our five senses. However, living a life of faith requires that we move beyond the limits of what we experience with our five senses to a place where faith in God gives us new vision. Then we gain a new ability to see more than our physical eyes can see and we begin to think like God thinks. When we think like God thinks, then we can see what He has intended for our lives. That only becomes possible when we rise above what is visible and see the good things that God has prepared for those who love Him.

Eventually, we begin to realize that what we can't see is much more important than what we can see. The root of visionary is vision, and where there is no vision, people perish. Look and live, but look with a renewed mind and reborn spirit. When we do this, we can see what our eyes cannot see. We can see that there is hope for each soul to be saved. We can see that it is possible for any sick to be well. We can see a bright future through our dark, cloudy days. We can see the best in the most dismal circumstances.

Faith sees clearly, focuses accurately, and interprets precisely. Walking by sight is blurry at best, but eyes full of faith have 20/20 vision.

CHAPTER 3

GOD HAS SPOKEN

✝

God spoke to young Emma through Mother Daisy Moore, one of the church mothers at Gethsemane Church of God in Christ in Altoona, PA. She told young Emma: *"God has a calling on your life."*

" God hath spoken once, twice have I heard this,
that power belongs to God.
Psalm 62:11

Evangelist Emma Creamer
"I have called you to preach!"

Evangelist Creamer believes it is very important for people to know the voice of God and how to discern when He is speaking to them. Throughout her life, God has spoken at various times either to her own heart directly or indirectly through a family member, a friend, a loved one, or a church member. She heard God's words clearly in her own heart when He said, *"I have called you to preach!"* Yet at other times, He spoke His words to her through others.

God speaks in many different ways to those who will listen. From Genesis 3 where Adam and Eve heard the voice of God in the cool of the day to Revelation 19 where His voice sounded like thunderings and many waters, God continues to speak to His creatures and His creation. As Elijah found out in I Kings 19, the voice of the Lord could not be found in the wind that had broken the rocks into pieces. Nor was His voice in the earthquake or the fire that followed the wind. Rather God spoke to the prophet Elijah in a still, small voice.

God spoke from the heavens after Jesus' baptism indicating to the hearers that He was pleased with His Son. He spoke with Moses from a bush that would not burn up, told Abram to get out of his father's country, and told Noah to build an ark to prepare for an impending flood in a land where it had rarely rained. He gives loving instructions to bless and protect. He called Samuel to be a priest and a prophet in the still of the night and answered David who inquired whether he should rise up and fight. On the road to Damascus, Paul heard His voice, and God's word proclaims repeatedly in Revelations instructions: *"he that hath an ear, let him hear."* Throughout the holy writ, God speaks to man instructing and guiding his affairs.

43

Sometimes we hear God in the quietness of the pre-dawn morning and sometimes in the silence of the middle of the night. His methods are many and varied. He uses angels and people. He spoke through a donkey and a detached hand that wrote on a wall. All we are required to do is just listen when He speaks. But how do we know for sure that we are hearing from God? There are times when every believer has had a doubt about whether they are really hearing from God. The world is so noisy that it can be hard to know if we are hearing the voice of God. Frequently God uses people to speak to us at times as He did when Emma's mother told her that God had chosen her and when Mother Moore said that God had a calling on her life. His voice is a knowing that whispers deep down in our hearts, and its stillness and smallness requires our undistracted attentiveness to hear what He says. Like the gentleness of His love, God's Spirit within confirms what He says and so does His word in the Holy Bible.

Every Good and Perfect Gift

Missionary Creamer was eventually appointed as a National Evangelist for the Church of God in Christ not too long after God called her to preach. As an evangelist, she traveled extensively, to large and small churches in places like Philadelphia, Baltimore, Cleveland, and Harrisburg. Sometimes she would have to minister at three different services on a Sunday – one in the morning, another in the afternoon, and a third one in the evening. She would drive from one engagement to another even though they were frequently in different cities that were miles apart.

God had also given her the gift of teaching, so she attended Baltimore City College and Towson State University in Maryland.

After that, she began working as a teaching assistant at Martin Luther King, Jr. Elementary School, where she formed a 75-voice gospel choir. God's gifts and guidance opened many doors for her, and many churches were requesting her to minister at their services.

As a national traveling evangelist, she would preach and sing on the weekends in those days. Creamer often arrived at school on Monday mornings worn out physically after a weekend full of ministering in various cities. Yet God's favor is truly amazing, and He gave her such great favor with her supervising principal that he told her she could have Mondays off because of the demands of the ministry on her weekend time! Again, God had spoken, only this time it was through a man, her principal! What teacher gets every Monday off? The teacher whom God favors because she wants to do His will. God is an amazingly kind Father, always loving and caring for us in unique ways. He speaks through and uses whomever He chooses, and what He says to and through others on our behalf guides us, helps us, and encourages us as we press toward His will.

Though the way seemed hard, Evangelist Creamer demonstrated an unusual determination to continue on the path that God had laid out for her. She faithfully juggled the conflicting demands of being a mother, traveling evangelist, and gospel recording artist. Of course she was very deeply devoted to her family. And, as is typical for working mothers, she prayerfully tried to balance the conflicting priorities. It was because of having to balance the demands of ministry with the responsibilities of motherhood that Evangelist Creamer took her children to Altoona to be with her mother. Mother Olive kept Yarah, Helena, and LeAndre for two years. She missed them immensely and her love for them compelled her to go to Altoona to be with them regularly.

I'll Fly Away

Evangelist Creamer had gone to her mother's to see her and the children on the night Mrs. Curry passed away. As is customary in families large or small, urban or rural, there had been a rift between her mother and one of Emma's sisters and the two had not communicated for a long time. Jesus taught in His sermon on the Mount that blessed are the peacemakers, so Evangelist Creamer took on the role of peacemaker and brought her sister to their mother's house praying that the estranged relationship between the two would be healed. Joyfully, Emma had been able to purchase this house for her mother, and thankfully she was now able to bring her mother and sister together through the ministry of reconciliation. They were all enjoying a wonderful time of fellowship together. But something strange happened while they visited and talked with each other. Emma suddenly felt very depressed and very sad. When she looked across the room at her mother, Mother Olive had silently and unnoticeably slipped into her eternal rest. No word to them and without warning at all, their mother had gone home peacefully to be with the Lord!

Twice Have I Heard

On their way to the hospital, Evangelist Creamer was very upset. She was distraught and quite distressed during the ambulance ride. Somewhat panicked, she attempted to strike a bargain with God. She had been willing to sing but she really didn't want the great responsibility of being a preacher. Though she had known for some time that God had called her to preach, she preferred singing and exercising her musical gifts. She was comfortable with that and thought that would be enough for her. Deep down inside, she knew she was running from the call to preach, and God knew it too. So she tried to strike a deal with God during the ambulance ride that night. She prayed in earnest a sincere prayer from her heart saying, "Lord if you spare my mother's life, I will preach for you." The Sovereign God who numbers both our days and the hairs on our very heads, whispered a reply whose finality seemed to thunder down deep in her heart. She heard God's answer to her clearly as the ambulance made its way to the hospital in Altoona. His reply to her was a whisper that seemed to roar back. God said, *"You will preach, if I don't spare life!"*

Once again, God had spoken. Her mother had now gone home to be with the Lord at the age of 66. It was hard to believe that the strong, humble lady who'd lent Emma her shoes had drawn her last breath. This was a very devastating time for Evangelist Creamer. Nevertheless, she had heard God's voice and knew she had to obey. No more could she run from God's real calling on her life. God was compelling her to preach. She knew she could no longer get away from His call. Her surrendered response to God's call finally came that night. Her response to God's call was settled and resolute. She told God at last, "I yield, I yield, I can't hold out any longer."

God is an expert planner and unerringly masterful at executing His plans completely and gloriously. His wisdom orchestrates the people and the circumstances so that the events and the people align perfectly with His sovereign will. God wanted Emma there that night – the night her mother made her transition from earth to glory. The events that seemingly had brought her there were simply the execution of God's sovereign plan for her life. He knew before it happened that she would attempt to strike a bargain with Him, and He knew that night her true surrender would begin. The evangelist could not deny the answer God had whispered back to her. Mother Curry was gone; her life had not been spared. Evangelist Creamer had her answer; she knew it was God.

God always guides us along the path we should go. He leads us along paths of righteousness for His name's sake. Hearing from God is critically important if we want to live a victorious life. If our own journey of faith is to be successful, we must develop our ability to hear God as Moses did, to hear from our spiritual leaders like Joshua did, and then share the word of God like John the Revelator did. As we listen intently, with our hearts stayed on Him, we find the answers to our questions, the solutions to our problems, and the hope or the help that we all need. Salvation and strength and health and peace are what we receive if we listen to Him. Joy and victory and blessings and love are ours if we'll listen carefully and prayerfully to the God we can trust.

Learning to discern and hear God's voice requires the help of His Holy Spirit and the application of God's word. The Spirit of God, the word of the Bible, and the Word made flesh (Jesus Christ) together will help you determine if the voice you hear is truly God's own. If it speaks of God's character and can be confirmed in God's word, we can trust it is God. If the message matches the message of Christ, we know it's God's voice and we can do as He says. If the person is saying what thus says the Lord, we'll find him or her in the written word of God.

It takes knowing God as our Father in a heart-to-heart

relationship with Him that is only made possible through our acceptance of Jesus, God's Son, in the pardon of our sins. It takes a relationship with God that is cultivated over time during which we grow in the grace and in the knowledge of our Lord and Savior Jesus Christ. It takes the infilling, indwelling presence of the Holy Spirit of God to rest, rule, and abide with us now and always. Time spent in personal study of God's word is our assurance that we're really hearing God's heart for our lives. LeRoy Eims said it well in his book entitled Be the Leader You Were Meant to Be. Eims says, "We must get into the Word, and the Word must get into us." It also takes our contact with those who are walking in communion with God and who meet the above criteria for fellowship and right relationship with Him. Then, we know it's His voice through another, and we can receive the man or woman of God, trusting that they're speaking as an ambassador for Him.

How blessed it is that Evangelist Creamer listened, she heard, and obeyed. It's good that she was learning to trust God's voice, letting Him direct her along her way. Her victories can also be attributed to her ability to listen to those through whom God spoke: her mother Olive Curry, Mother Russ and Mother Moore, Rev. Rainey and Dr. Howard to name just a few. God sometimes uses others to speak His own words to our lives. God will speak to those who will listen, hear, heed, and obey. If we'll hear, He'll use someone in our lives to speak His words to us. We only need listening ears and obedient hearts. Take note below of a few key times in Evangelist Creamer's life when God's voice was directing and leading the way on the road to victory in her journey of faith.

GOD IS SPEAKING

HOW IT HAPPENED	WHAT GOD SAID
Through her mother, Ms. Olive Curry, when she was a young girl	"God has chosen you"
Through Mother Daisy Moore, church mother, Gethsemane COGIC	"God has a calling on your life"
Through church Mother Vera Russ	"Pastor" Creamer
In 1973 at her home one night	"I have called you to preach"
Through Rev. Ross B. Rainey	"God told me to put you in preparation"
While she was in preparation	"There is an effectual door open to you"
During the court battle after Rev. Rainey's death	"Don't fight, just praise Me."
After the court's decision in her favor	"You're free"
After her offer for a prospective building on Phila. Pike was rejected	"You may lose on the front, but you'll gain on the back."
In the truck warehouse before it was renovated into the Cathedral	"Offer him $175,000 cash"
In her car after offering $175,000 for the truck warehouse (the asking price was $350,000)	"And I shall supply all your needs"
In a dream before the church restoration	"You're tall enough"
In her apartment in response to her prayer for the name of her new church	"The Cathedral of Fresh Fire"

Earning the anointing of God involves being able to discern God's voice and understand the completeness of His message to you. Later on as a pastor, Creamer would occasionally say that "God is speaking," and the tone of her statement always caused her listeners to tune in to precisely what God was saying to them. Remember, she had learned to listen as a little girl. Her own mother had carried God's message for her as did Mother Daisy Moore, Mother Vera Russ, Elder Ross Rainey and others. Discerning God's voice and hearing Him through others is vitally important. Whether He whispers a message in the middle of the night or cries aloud from a Sunday morning pulpit, Evangelist Creamer learned the invaluable skill of hearing and heeding the awesome and precious voice of God.

After Christ was baptized, Luke 3:22 records that *"a voice came from heaven, which said, Thou art my beloved Son; in thee I am well pleased."* Christ was then led into the wilderness to be tempted by the devil. In the same way, Evangelist Creamer was about to be led into her own type of wilderness experience. She could not have imagined the fiery trial she was about to face just ahead on her journey. But thank God she had already become familiar with the sound of God's voice. Danger and peril drew near unawares and a major life's trial crouched near at her door. If ever she needed the Lord before, the stately evangelist surely and undoubtedly would really need Him now.

LIFE LESSON 3
God Has Spoken

It is vitally important to have a healthy relationship with God and to understand the message He is communicating to us. He communicates with us through His word, through people, through circumstances, and through His still small voice in our hearts. As our relationship with God deepens, we begin to know His voice and a stranger we will not follow.

This world is way too noisy and full of distractions. If we do not turn off the noise of this world at times, and tune in to our God, we could miss His divine guidance for our lives. Get quiet, be still, and listen to God. Listen intently and intentionally. Purpose sometimes not to speak during prayer but only to listen to God. God's still, small voice becomes clear as a bell.

It is by God's purpose and design that we have been created with two ears and one mouth. This means, of course, that we should do twice as much listening as speaking. There is a certain finality to the words of our God. He says what He means and means what He says. Pay close attention to His holy word in the Bible. As He helps you, apply it to your daily life. The late Pastor Horace Shepard, Sr. (West Oak Lane Church of God, Philadelphia, PA) was quite a profound and prolific preacher who wanted his people to not only hear God, but he wanted them to do what God says as well. Pastor Shepard would frequently end his sermons by saying, "Now put that thing in shoe leather and walk it."

CHAPTER 4

DON'T FIGHT JUST PRAISE HIM

✝

God's directions to Evangelist Creamer after the church
people sued her in court *"Don't fight, just praise Me!"*

"For we wrestle not against flesh and blood . . .
Ephesians 6:12

The Weary Shall Be at Rest

In 1991, after a brief illness, the late, great Reverend Ross B. Rainey, went home to be with the Lord. His passing away seemed as gentle and peaceful as his own life of ministry had been. His death shocked Wilmington, however, and hundreds mourned at the passing of one who had shown such love for God and His people. He had built up his church in Wilmington, preached, prayed for, counseled, and helped so many during his years of service unto God. The gentle preacher with a quiet spirit had now gone on to his eternal rest. The legacy of his ministry was a people who loved God and would go to great lengths of sacrifice and service for the cause of Christ. That was the foundation of his great ministry, and his legacy continues to live on in the hearts and the spirits of his members and of the generations that followed even to this present day. Rev. Rainey left his devoted wife, Thelma, to mourn him as well as his spiritual daughter, Emma, and a congregation who had loved him as much as he had loved them. He had earned the respect of so many during the course of his ministry, and his passing changed Evangelist Creamer's life in a way she could have never imagined.

Rev. Rainey had always let Evangelist Creamer know that he wanted her to lead the church when he was gone. Evangelist knew that but not many others shared in this knowledge. When a pastor indicates he wishes his spiritual daughter to take over as the pastor of the church, the expectation is that his daughter will take his place as the pastor. Reasonable expectation says that there will be no hindrance to the fulfillment of his desire especially since he has demonstrated his own faithfulness to God and shown love, care, and concern for his church members.

In addition, if the pastor had been faithful to the Bible and had laid down his life for the sheep, certainly his followers would want to fulfill his wishes. Once Rainey's wishes were divulged after his decease, however, doubts arose because of the lack of written evidence. Those doubts became questions that eventually evolved into outright opposition. But, why would anyone want to oppose the late pastor's wishes? What would be the basis of a movement to reject the chosen heir? Whose idea was it to fight against the desires of the man who proved himself faithful to the call? What controversy could motivate the uprising that took place when it came time for the passing of the baton from the late Rev. Ross B. Rainey to the successor he chose, Evangelist Emma Creamer? The answer to these questions sparked a fiery trial for the daughter who had served faithfully alongside her spiritual father – a man who believed that God could use anybody. He had taught it and lived it during his tenure as pastor and had put Evangelist Creamer "in preparation" in accordance with the divine directions He had received from the Lord.

But Evangelist Emma Creamer, who was the first of Elder Rainey's "Five Spiritual Daughters," was chosen by God, and not necessarily by man. After Rainey's death, when it was time for her promotion as Rainey's successor, opposition to her promotion began to surface. Many were opposed to a female as pastor, so some whom she had ministered to did not support her. She had preached, sang, played, and evangelized, but the uprising was real in spite of all she'd done under Rainey's leadership. The battle for leadership of the church ensued, and the bitter struggle ended up in a courtroom. Rev. Rainey wanted Evangelist Creamer to follow him. But many of the members of his church did not.

Her opponents emerged and began to fight. A woman could evangelize, or teach, or do the work of a missionary, but a woman as pastor was generally frowned upon.

Many others wanted Evangelist Creamer as their pastor. The late Dr. L. Ramona Howard, Elder Carolyn Martin-Pettaway, Elder Delnora Roberts, and Elder Tammy Lindsay led the way in support of Evangelist Creamer, and this group along with Creamer were known as "The Five Daughters" of Rev. Ross B. Rainey. These ladies had already distinguished themselves as faithful servants under Rev. Rainey's leadership, and they continued to serve amidst the growing turmoil after his death. They were devoted to God and were determined to support Evangelist Creamer during what was to become the most difficult challenge of her life.

It was during this time and at this moment of challenge in her life when I first met Evangelist Creamer. I visited their church one Sunday morning and saw Evangelist Creamer and her praise team conducting an awesome worship and praise service. I had moved to escape from drama and trauma in my own life, and the high level of worship and praises to God there was exactly what I needed. I saw no traces of a church divided, rather what I experienced was a great love for God and a desire to worship and praise Him because He alone is worthy. As a newcomer, I did not see or sense even a trace of evidence that Evangelist Creamer and her supporters were facing serious opposition there. I have always been amazed at that fact. I did not know about her problems until much later. No one spoke about the struggle openly. All I observed from Evangelist Creamer and her team was that they were very serious about worship, about praise, and about honoring God. Years later, I learned that during that time, some members found themselves in an emotional tug-of-war inside their own hearts. They were torn and halting between two opinions. On the one hand, they loved Evangelist Creamer and were grateful for all that she'd done to help Elder Rainey and the church. On the other hand, they were hearing others who did not want Evangelist Creamer to lead.

Elder Rainey was gone; his contributions and his legacy would never be forgotten. But some of the members did not want what he wanted. They had been blessed as Evangelist Creamer ministered in service. She had sung, she had preached – she had cooked, she had cared. They had left many services uplifted, encouraged, strengthened, and renewed. They had received the benefit of Evangelist Creamer's God-given gifts again and again.

While Rainey lived, her ministry during services had brought them to their feet, to their knees, and sometimes to the floor. Her messages had elicited among them tears of joy and tears of hope. Still, the congregation was split — some wanting Evangelist Creamer as pastor, some did not. The small church building could not contain the fight inside.

Her opponents made a bold move and filed a lawsuit against her. This would prove to be the showdown of showdowns for the statuesque evangelist who was chosen by God. In addition to the question of who would take over as the next pastor, there was also a dispute about who actually owned the church building because the evangelist had been instrumental in fund raising and church remodeling efforts. The disagreement took Evangelist Creamer to a local courtroom in the biggest battle of her life. The next pastor would have to be decided by a judge. Little did she know that the process would eventually require them to appear in court three times. Evangelist Creamer was now in the fight of her life. God had chosen her. The people had not. Rainey had prepared her. His members were rejecting her as their next leader. How can two walk together unless they agree? The age-old tactic of the enemy to divide and conquer was now working among them, and only God could deliver them now.

Sadly, all of this drama left her no time to mourn the death of her spiritual father. She had to be strong at a time when people are at their lowest and weakest. The man who'd brought her to his home and his church and helped her grow into her ministry robes had not only died and left her, but he'd left her with the fight of her life. At a time when she should have been able to mourn Rainey's loss, Evangelist Creamer had to control her emotions enough to prepare her defense. A courageous woman with an indomitable spirit, Evangelist Creamer and her loyalists were given a prime opportunity to demonstrate the fruit of the Spirit, self-control. About 50 members believed in her leadership and decided to stand with her as she contended for the legacy God had chosen for her.

Pastor reported that emotions ran hot and tensions were high as the divided congregation continued to meet together on Sundays for service. In one incident, as Evangelist Creamer was called on to minister a song during service, an opponent snatched the microphone from her hand. It was now apparent that they would not be able to worship together. The community of their fellowship had died with Elder Rainey. The unity of their faith had been stolen from them by his death. The opposition against Evangelist Creamer as their next pastor was undeniably and painfully real.

Many viewed the opposition as completely unwarranted. She was undoubtedly anointed and unmistakably equipped, but the uproar against her becoming the next pastor became more and more obvious as the weeks went by. This was a difficult test and a terrible trial for Creamer that could not be prayed away, they couldn't shout it away, and the great evangelist herself could not even preach it away. They were forced to a showdown with the dreaded enemy: a divided congregation and the difficulty of determining who would stay and who would not. The worse had now come true for the lively congregation. They were born again, but the adversary would now attempt to destroy their faith – their faith in each other if not their faith in God.

This was a major test of their ability to apply the word to their present actions. Many times they'd heard Rev. Rainey preach that a house divided against itself cannot stand. They had heard, but could they heed? Could they pass the challenging test of remaining unified when a spirit of division was attacking them? They'd heard the sermons about unity and had shouted amen, but could they now find a way to turn their shouts of assent into actions of unity around this challenging cause? It's great to hear an inspiring message preached from the pulpit. But sometimes it can seem nearly impossible to actually live out His word. The word challenges us to be really true to God and to do what the Bible tells us to do. That's sometimes very difficult for us humans when we think we know what is right and believe that others are wrong. Christ prayed in John 17:21, *"That they all may be one; as thou, Father, art in me, and I in thee, that they also may be one in us . . ."* We all need the grace of God to allow His word to change us so that we don't just talk the talk but we actually walk the walk of newness in Christ.

The challenge of unity was too great, and the battle ensued with Creamer's opponents refusing to allow her to be their pastor while her supporters strengthened their support of her cause. Evangelist Creamer had worked so hard alongside Rev. Rainey. How could Creamer and her followers just leave? She'd grown up under Rainey; he'd mentored her and worked diligently to prepare her for the task of leading the flock. She'd obeyed and sacrificed and worked faithfully with him. Could she now just quietly blend into the background? Could she just walk away after all those years of preparation? What about the renovations she'd sponsored to beautify the building? What about the sermons she'd preached, the songs she had sung? What about the hundreds she'd ministered to there? Had that all been for naught? She was accustomed to ministering to others and setting her own needs aside. So, she hid her own pain during that time, and no one knew how she was hurting inside or the tears she cried night after night.

Patience With the Process

She and her supporters had to endure the painstaking process of going to court three times, and each time she reports that she felt and knew that God was with them. Evangelist Creamer noted that each time they had to appear in court, she sensed the presence of God. He had always been true to His holy word, and she knew He would not let her down now. Creamer began to do her best to withstand the fight. She'd been called and chosen, and the time of her preparation had ended. It was now her time to lead God's people, and she determined to do exactly that. For God and for Rev. Rainey, she took a stand against her opponents.

A fighter by nature and a woman who knew how to stand for a cause, Evangelist Creamer was not a stranger to winning battles. She'd learned to play the piano without a single lesson on a broken piano that had only two keys. As a child, she had led a choir of adults and later formed her own gospel group and recorded albums. She knew how to hold her own in a hostile world as a minority woman and a committed disciple of Christ. Standing six feet tall, her stature offered a commanding presence that exuded authority and control. Evangelist Creamer did not mince words, and there was no mistaking her authority or her ability to straighten things out that needed it. But now her authority was being challenged and tested. God knew what He had placed inside of Creamer, and He wanted her to know it too. He showed her one afternoon during noonday prayer that with God on her side, she could conquer any foe.

As Administrative Assistant, Evangelist Creamer was responsible for leading the weekly Noonday Prayer Service. She knew and believed that an active prayer life is a vitally important part of new life in Christ Jesus, and praying corporately with other believers provides both the strength of fellowship as well as the power of agreement. Their meetings were always blessed by the presence and the power of God. On one occasion, Bishop T. D. Jakes of the Potter's House in Dallas arrived in their meeting unexpectedly. He ministered to them on the topic of prayer, exhorting them to always keep praying and to remain faithful in prayer because it is a critical aspect of achieving the victory in our lives. Evangelist Creamer listened to Bishop Jakes that day and continued to remain faithful, always showing up to lead the weekly noonday prayer services.

The Devil Comes to Church

On one occasion during prayer service, she and a few other saints gathered for prayer. The prayer got started, and as Evangelist Creamer ministered up front, the door came open at the back of the church. The fiery evangelist could not believe what she saw next. Something very large and very dark came through the door and began crawling ever so slowing – almost inch by inch – up the center aisle of the church. At first, she could not determine what (or who) it was that continued to crawl ever so slowly, dragging itself closer and closer towards Evangelist Creamer up front. She was startled, confused, and fear began to rise in her chest. Nothing like this had ever happened to her before. Her heart began pounding, and thoughts flooded her mind. What should she do? What could she do? How should she handle this? What should she say? Fear was trying to take over and swallow up her faith. As they all watched in horror and disbelief, Creamer breathed a silent prayer to God. And then God's word came clearly into her spirit reminding her that God had not given her a spirit of fear.

The dark, ugly figure continued crawling slowly and painstakingly up the aisle like an alligator preparing for a vicious attack. As he came closer, they saw that it was a large, dark-skinned man. When he finally reached the front, at first he just crouched at Evangelist Creamer's feet. Then he got up from the floor and glared at her with evil and piercing eyes. The burly man then walked right past her and up the steps into the church's pulpit area. Everyone stood still as they watched and prayed and wondered what would happen next. The man then turned around, came down from the pulpit, walked over to Evangelist Creamer, and stood face to face with her. After a long silence, he finally spoke. Almost grunting he said, "You are a woman of God!"

He then turned, walked down the center aisle and out of the church without harming a single soul! Of course, they all began to praise God, clapping and thanking Him for hearing their prayers and protecting them from the potential attack. God had shown the Evangelist through this event that, though the enemy may threaten her, God would hear her and answer her and protect her. Her confrontation with the enemy during that noonday prayer meeting was a lesson for her that whatever she would face, God would see her through. She'd been fearful and unsure for a moment while it was all happening, but in the end she would endure and win.

Sometimes God sends an almost prophetic type of encouragement for believers and leaders who are sold out to Him. They may be facing danger on the road just ahead, but God will always be there to protect them, defend them, and cause them to win. The important principle is not to give in to fear. *"For God hath not given us the spirit of fear; but of power, and of love, and of a sound mind."* II Timothy 1:7.

Yes, she was facing the ominous court fight, but God showed her that day during noonday prayer, that in the end, she was going to emerge victorious. The enemy may look very scary, and fear may even rise in your heart. But God had reminded her that the battle was not hers; it was His. Yes, she had a multitude of questions about the outcome of the lawsuit against her. What was going to happen to her and her followers? Would God cause them to win? Will the court rule in their favor? Did they stand any chance at all of winning the victory? The answers would come, but right now she just had to wait. Their faith in God is all they had. They did not yet know if it would be all they needed.

Hurt, confused, and ready for justification, she readied herself and her supporters for the series of three different days in court. They'd spent about $50,000 beautifying the church, and as a good steward of God's business, Evangelist Creamer could not just walk away. God in His great faithfulness was with her throughout this ordeal. She never lost her faith or trust in Him. The weapon had been formed against her – she was being taken to court. But she herself knew the end of that verse: *"No weapon formed against you shall prosper and every tongue that rises against you in judgment, you shall condemn for this is your heritage as a servant of the Lord, and their righteousness is of me, saith the Lord."* (Isaiah 54:17) She knew the verse and had preached it to others many times, and now she was experiencing it first hand. God is true to His holy word. He means what He says and has said what He means. No weapon means none. Every tongue means every one. Creamer was about to experience the living word of God in its complete power and virtuous truth. For right in the midst of the court battle and the days that followed, God did a miraculous thing: He spoke. God spoke a phrase to Evangelist Creamer that became branded in her consciousness. A simple phrase that changed the course of her ministry and the path of the rest of her life. God spoke a phrase that impacted her supporters and the generations of them that followed.

To help Evangelist Creamer and her supporters, to ease the pain of the fray, to calm their troubled hearts, and to soothe their minds, God spoke. He told Evangelist Creamer very simply one day during it all, *"Don't fight, just praise Me! The battle is not yours; it belongs to God."* That was it! That was exactly what she had needed to hear – a word from the Lord to see them through! "Don't fight, just praise Me" became indelibly etched into her mind, her spirit, her thoughts, her actions, and her ministry. She told her supporters what God had said: *"Don't fight, just praise Me."* It caught on immediately. God's Spirit etched it into their hearts, their spirits, their thoughts, and their actions, too. Praise became their first and foremost activity, their top priority, their overriding purpose. They began to praise God as never before. They praised God with their singing, with their music, with their mouths, with their hands, with their bodies, and with their lives. Praise became the weapon that it had been for the Israelites in Judges 1:1-2:

"Now after the death of Joshua it came to pass that the children of Israel asked the Lord, saying, Who shall go up for us against the Canaanites first to fight against them? And the Lord said, Judah shall go up: behold I have delivered the land into his hand."

Judah means praise, so the Israelites sent the praisers first. And likewise, so did Evangelist Creamer, teach her supporters to praise God first. Their focus turned away from the courtroom and turned toward how much more can they praise God for who He is and for what He is about to do. They stopped fighting in their hearts and their spirits and began to lift up the high praises of God as they had never done it before. Creamer exhorted them to show love to her opponents. They were not permitted to be rude or impolite, but she taught them to "be sweet" to the people and send up high praises to God. And that is exactly what they did. They praised God as loud as they could. They praised God with unending gratitude, with exuberant faith each in their own way. The praise would cause some to run during worship services. Others would leap for joy. Many others shouted or danced. It is a kind of praise that words can't explain – the kind that pleases God because it comes from a broken spirit and a contrite heart.

The praise became so powerful that people became undignified, uninhibited, and unashamed of the way in which they praised God. To illustrate how pervasive the praises became, I remember one particularly powerful service that I attended during that time. It may have been a Friday service because I was dressed somewhat casually that day and wore my hair in a bun on top of my head. But what I do vividly recall is that the praises of God broke forth and took over the service. People would often faint under the anointing and power of the praise without having anyone touch or lay hands on them. I remember that when I began to praise God, I completely forgot about everything around me. I was consumed by God's praises and somehow ended up on the floor. The ministry leaders would always assist those who were overcome during these times of high praise. When I finally calmed down and began to get up, I discovered that Elder Tammy Lindsay had been assisting me. (Elder Lindsay had been with Evangelist Creamer in ministry for a number of years.) What is amusing now in retrospect years later is that the moment of praise had been so pervasive and all-consuming that I had "shouted" myself right out of my pony tail holder and the neat hair bun on my head had now become a very messy pony "turd!" When I caught a glimpse of Elder Lindsay, she had a knowing look on her face and seemed to not even notice my disheveled look. She seemed to have understood exactly how I had felt praising God without restraint. Today we would laugh, but back then we did not. I later found my ponytail holder on the floor, picked it up, and sat back down. I will always remember that service because it was my first experience with praising God without restraint.

We gave God the kind of praise that is a sacrifice under difficult circumstances. Ours was a praise that is cleansing. Our praise got God's attention. He inhabits and lives in the praise, so He was there the whole time. Evangelist Creamer and her original supporters were hurting and waiting, yet they offered praise in sacrifice, in obedience, and in faith. Her new ministry was being birthed and covered in this highly unusual and all-encompassing kind of praise.

Let God Arise and His Enemies Be Scattered

The praises of God carried the ministry into an overwhelming victory. Finally on the last of the three days they had to appear in court, the judge ruled in Evangelist Creamer's favor! God had fought the battle and given them the resounding victory. Thank God that the battle was finally over, and they had won! The hard trial was finally over and when the dust cleared, Evangelist Creamer's ministry emerged victoriously. God had granted her favor because: *"For though we walk in the flesh, we do not war after the flesh: For the weapons of our warfare are not carnal, but mighty through God to the pulling down of strongholds."* II Cor. 10:3-4. Their prayers had been answered. They had obeyed the directions not to fight and just to praise God and their praise propelled them to a sweeping victory. The court decision included granting Evangelist Creamer the most favorable time for Sunday worship: Sunday morning. God made them into more than conquerors because they did not fight back in the carnal sense. They had used the spiritual weapon of praise, and praise won the day. Hallelujah is the highest praise – and faithful God came through for them victoriously! To God be the glory, Emmanuel, our God, He is with us.

After the court victory, the praise that we gave to God attracted many new members, and the ranks of Creamer's followers increased. The phrase: *"Don't fight, just praise Him"* became the foundation of her new ministry – a ministry built on praise. Addicts were delivered during the praise. People were healed of diseases like AIDS and cancer because we continued to praise. There were many testimonies of financial miracles as a result of our determination to always give God the praise.

This new level of praise became the vehicle that transported Creamer's ministry to the next level in God. Praise became the hallmark of her ministry and word spread throughout the region that Evangelist Creamer's ministry takes praise to another level and another dimension. Her ministry became renown for its unparalleled level of praise. We were not just praising God with our whole hearts, but we were praising God with our whole hearts, souls, minds, and strength. Praise is what we did, and Emmanuel, our God, showed that He was with us. Evangelist Creamer sang many comforting and uplifting songs during those days including this one entitled "Emmanuel, Our God, Is With Us:

> ♫ *God is with us*
> *He is with us*
> *Emmanuel, our God, is with us*
> *Everywhere we go*
> *This one thing we know*
> *Emmanuel, our God, is with us*

Stand Fast in the Liberty Wherewith Christ Has Made You Free

For a while, Evangelist Creamer and her supporters continued to meet in the same building with their opponents. Creamer and her group held their praise services on Sunday mornings, while her opponents were forced to meet in the afternoons. Before long, however, God spoke once again. She'd won the victory through God and His praises, and He was now ready to take her to another place in Him: to her own building. The words He now spoke to Creamer were, *"You are free."* Free? Free to go? Free to go where? Where would they go? They had no other place to meet, and they did not have enough money to buy a place of their own. Nonetheless, it was clear to Creamer, that she and her supporters were being released to go. Her perilous journey had exposed her to some of the worst opposition and the deepest hurt she had ever faced. The battle had been won with praise and faith, obedience and trust. Her faith had brought her on thus far, and she knew that her faith would lead her home.

Becoming conformed to the image of Christ happens to us believers on our journeys of faith. Gradually, we learn not to fight with the weapons of the flesh that are carnal and ineffective. Our Savior has exemplified for us the behavior required when we are attacked by evil. He forgave; so must we. He endured without self-defense; so must we. He yielded to God's will; and so must we. It's never easy during times of intense battle to crucify our flesh or to mortify the deeds of our bodies. We'd prefer to hit back when we've been hit. We'd rather retaliate when we've been hurt. The most challenging times for believers are those times when we must be doers of the word and not hearers only. The power that we gain through our faith, trust, and obedience to God's word is unstoppable and insurmountable during times of attack. That power is released when our love for God allows us to yield to His way and forsake our own.

Herein lies the beauty of this overwhelming victory for soon-to-be Pastor Emma Creamer. Her obedience to God's word and her refusal to fight in the carnal sense brought forth the power of God and His victory on her behalf. She was demonstrating Romans 12:21: *"Be not overcome of evil; but overcome evil with good."* Praise birthed her ministry and praise caused it to grow. The praise was like a powerful magnet that attracted many others. The number of members was increasing, and they could not and would not stop praising God. Elder Delnora Roberts summarized it well in the title of one of her sermons, <u>You Have Two Times To Praise God – When You Feel Like It and When You Don't!</u> The praises of Pastor Creamer's people propelled them forward on the journey of faith. A ministry of praisers is what they became and a ministry of miracles is what they obtained.

Evangelist Creamer was an avid tennis player who was difficult to beat. Her victory in court was like winning a challenging tennis match against a very formidable opponent. God's people always end up being triumphant and victorious. He always causes us to triumph in Christ. Now, with the painful court battle behind her, God would now lead her on to a much bigger, much better, much higher place of praise – to the place of a pastor for which she was chosen.

LIFE LESSON 4
God's Praise Shall Continually Be In My Mouth

Every battle of the believer belongs to God, and we win every time we allow God to fight for us and give us the victory. We must follow God's instructions and obey His will, and when we do that we always win.

If God instructs us not to fight, but just to praise Him, then that is what we must do. In fact, praising God when we are faced with an enemy's attack keeps our focus exactly where it needs to be: on God who made us more than conquerors and causes us always in all things to triumph in Christ Jesus. The principle to remember here is to follow God's instructions explicitly, and as we keep the focus on His power and goodness, we will conquer every foe.

Jonathan Edwards, great preacher, theologian, and philosopher, provides an appropriate conclusion for us in the title of one of his many prolific sermons. Edwards underscored the absolute primacy of praise and provided for us a fitting reminder of its significance in the life of believers when he entitled one of his 18th century sermons: "Praise, One of the Chief Employments of Heaven!" In essence, we were created for worship, and our job in this life, principally and primarily, is praise!

CHAPTER 5

EFFECTUAL DOORS

✝

Original lyrics by Pastor Creamer:
"Zion is calling me to a higher place of praise!"

"For a great and effectual door is opened unto me . . ."
I Corinthians 16:9

Evangelist Creamer and her followers had won the court fight, but the fulfillment of the victory would require even more of her now. She'd survived the heartbreaking court battle and the painful church split. With God nothing is impossible, and now this same incredible God would guide her from her place of preparation to a much bigger, better, and higher place of praise. Creamer would soon discover that the higher place was the place of a pastor.

Evangelist Creamer had been living Philippians 4:13-14 ever since she'd left Altoona. Her circumstances had required her to press. The pressure of her opposition caused her to have the kind of determination the Apostle Paul characterized when he said: *"I press toward the mark for the prize of the high calling of God that is in Christ Jesus."* His press was born out of the pressure and the opposition placed on him in his various missionary journeys. The pressure of the battle that was fought and won with praise had now birthed in her a new and more courageous determination to press her way through. The high calling which had been spoken over her life back in Altoona many, many years before would now come to fulfillment. Her mother had told her that God had chosen her. And He had. Mother Daisy Moore said that God had a calling on her life. And He did. And Mother Vera Russ had called her "Pastor Creamer." And that is exactly what God was now ready to do. The truth of these prophetic utterances would now be fulfilled.

In this new life we have in Christ, there are times when we must move in obedient, child-like faith. Abraham had to leave his hometown and familiar surroundings, and Moses did too. Joshua also left from where he started, and the Apostle Paul journeyed in faith and trust in God. Pushed forward and carried along by the Spirit of God, these Biblical examples of journeying in faith show us how to carry on God's mission by moving with Him. There were places of promise that they had to see. There were people God loved who had to hear about Him. There were blessings in their future that compelled them to go. At these times, faith acts as a magnet, drawing one forth. Its pull is powerful and irresistible. Faith can propel an individual out of their comfort zone and into what would seem like a danger zone except for the fact that the safest place to be is exactly where God wants us to be.

A life of faith requires the kind of faith in God that trusts Him implicitly and takes Him at His word. God is experienced deeply in places of abiding faith – faith that He will carry us through. He is a God of exceeding great and precious promises who not only makes the promises but fulfills them too. Though he was shipwrecked, imprisoned, beaten, and stoned in his missionary travels, Paul continued to spread the gospel anyway declaring boldly in Philippians 4:13: *"I can do all things through Christ which strengtheneth me."* The apostle's example is a powerful motivator for any missionary turned evangelist who is soon to become a pastor.

God was now leading Evangelist Creamer out of the place she'd known and loved and worked tirelessly to build up. The move would require more faith than ever. Where would she go? Her and those 50+ faithful followers – where would they go? These questions were yet to be answered. All she knew was that she had to press on. She had come this far by faith, and she already knew that she can do all things through Christ who strengthens her. So Evangelist Creamer pressed forward in unwavering faith and uncompromising obedience and began her search for a new place to worship, and a higher place of praise. She knew where to turn for help. She had sung the words many times. Where could she go but to the Lord?

🎵 *Where could I go?*
Tell me, where could I go?
Needing a refuge for my soul
Needing a friend to help me in the end
Where could I go but to the Lord?

Promotion Comes From God

The next steps Evangelist Creamer took on her journey of faith would take her to ordination as elder and installation as pastor. God decided that she had earned this elevation. Notice God's opinion on this in Psalm 75:6-7: *"For promotion cometh neither from the east, nor from the west, nor from the south. But God is the judge: he putteth down one, and setteth up another."* Evangelist Creamer had become qualified to carry this title and to fulfill this role. Her faith, her obedience, her trials, and her turmoil had earned her this anointing.

The anointing comes upon a leader in two ways. First, they must spend time and experience in faithful obedience and relationship with God. Years of service and sacrifice are required. They must have tenure in Christ and a resume of victories in Him that can only happen over many years spent in faithful service to Him. There are no shortcuts to this, and God is not mocked. Observe in your world the age and the stage of those whose lives are like written epistles that can be read of all men. The overwhelming majority are not very young in years (though many are hopefully very young at heart). It is God alone who determines our times and our seasons. He promotes when He decides. It is His choice, and His alone. The young can be trained and should be provided opportunities to serve, but the anointing that destroys yokes and removes burdens is earned through years spent in prayer and faithful service, overcoming life's tests and trials while remaining true to God as He molds and shapes us on the His potter's wheel.

Second, the anointing to walk in an office of ministry is transferred officially by the laying on of hands of the presbytery. I Timothy 4:14 says: *"Neglect not the gift that is in thee, which was given thee by prophecy, with the laying on of hands of the presbytery."* When she was only 11 years old, Evangelist Creamer was asked to represent the Altoona District of the Church of God in Christ organization by singing and playing the piano at a convocation in Philadelphia. At the convocation, she got in the prayer line, and Bishop Mason, founder of the Church of God in Christ, laid his hands on her, and she fainted under the anointing and the power of God. Years later, she attended a service in Orlando, Florida. Pastor Benny Hinn led the service, and when Evangelist Creamer went up for prayer, Pastor Hinn laid his hands on her and again she fainted under the powerful anointing and presence of God. God had been preparing her all along, and He used powerful people to transfer the anointing to her that promoted her from Evangelist Creamer to Pastor Creamer.

To receive her promotion, Evangelist Creamer traveled all the way to Cleveland, Ohio to be ordained as an elder and installed as the overseer of her new ministry by Bishop J. DeLano Ellis, II. The day she was ordained God again crossed her path with Bishop T. D. Jakes who delivered the sermon for her ordination service that day. Bishop Ralph Dennis, a friend and mentor, joined the others in confirming her promotion and her calling to the pastorate. Bishop Dennis told her she had "God's signature" on her life. He explained that this meant she carried all of the five-fold ministry gifts of apostle, evangelist, prophet, pastor, and teacher as mentioned in Ephesians 4:11. All of this confirmed her elevation into the pastorate and represented the fulfillment of prophecies that had been spoken over her life over the years. The early prophecies were now being fulfilled, and the laying on of hands confirmed God's will to elevate her to the office of pastor. The effectual door was truly open, and her promotion had finally and thankfully come.

When she was ordained to the pastorate, seven faithful supporters were ordained as deacons in her new ministry at the same time. They were: Carolyn Martin, Kirk Clay, Jacqueline Rivers, Geri Nolan, Oreta Richardson, Randall Stickney, and Elijah Roberts. Deaconess Carolyn Martin (now Elder Carolyn Martin-Pettaway) proved to be an exceptionally faithful assistant to Pastor Creamer as she assumed her new role as pastor. Deaconess Martin welcomed Pastor into her home, providing a place for Pastor Creamer to stay while she was in Wilmington ministering so that she would not have to travel from Baltimore to Wilmington every week. Martin became a dear friend and confidante who has worked faithfully with Pastor Creamer for more than 30 years helping her build the ministry.

Along with other key and instrumental people, this group

formed the foundation of this new and exciting ministry, and onward and upward they climbed. Together, they planned for the day they would leave that small building in Wilmington. To them, it truly felt like an Exodus experience as if they were leaving Egypt like the Israelites and proceeding toward the promised land. In fact, they planned the eventful day when they would actually leave their old building and termed it "The Exodus March." They decided to all wear red on that day to symbolize the color of the blood that was placed on the lintels and doorposts of the Israelites houses on the night of the Passover in Exodus 12:21-22. And for them, the color red also represented the color of the blood of Jesus, the Lamb who was slain before the foundation of the world (Revelation 13:8). So these 50 or so followers of Christ and supporters of Pastor Creamer decided that they would boldy and courageously take their step of faith and obey God's leading away from their familiar place to the place of God's promise, provision, and peace.

Seek and You Shall Find

As soon as she knew that God wanted her to leave, Pastor Creamer began praying and preparing. Seeking the Lord in earnest for where to go next was the cry of her heart and her effectual and fervent prayer. During this time, she received a phone call from the pastor of Ebenezer Baptist Church in Wilmington. Knowing that Pastor Creamer was in the process of searching for a building to worship, he told her that there was a building on sale across from his church and that she should hurry over to take a look at it. Pastor Creamer wasted no time getting over to the location. It was a large truck warehouse of more than 18,000 square feet with an additional piece of land across the street from it. This was it! Immediately she knew that she wanted the building. Inside, the floors were covered with a thick layer of trucking grease and grimy dirt, and the beamed ceiling was covered with soot. But Pastor knew in her heart that this was her church, and she wanted it nonetheless! The warehouse owner's son was there that day. He told Pastor Creamer that his father wanted $350,000 for the building and another $75,000 for the land across from it. Pastor Creamer, knowing she did not have that kind of money, walked into the large open area of the warehouse and prayed to God letting him know that she wanted this building. God impressed on her heart these words: *"Offer him $175,000 cash."* Pastor Creamer turned around, went back to the owner's son, and told him: "I'll offer you $175,000 cash." The son's reply to Pastor Creamer was that he would have to speak with his father. Pastor advised him to contact the church secretary with his answer, and the owner's son promised to get back to her within two weeks. Before leaving the warehouse, Pastor told the owner's son: "Well you go ahead and talk to your father, because I've already talked to mine!"

God's Abundant Supply

On the way home in her car after that meeting, God spoke in Pastor's heart once again. His reassuring words to her were: *"And I shall supply all of your needs."* Her heart was so encouraged that tears came to her eyes as she told Dr. Howard what God had said. She drove home to her apartment (which was located about five minutes from the warehouse). About 20 minutes later, Pastor's phone rang. It was the church secretary, Deaconess Carolyn Martin. Deaconess Martin asked Pastor if she was sitting down. Pastor Creamer sat down. Deaconess Martin then told Pastor Creamer that the warehouse owner had accepted her offer of $175,000 cash! Martin added that they had also agreed to give her the empty lot across the street free of charge! What a miracle! Glory to God! God gave Pastor such tremendous favor that the price of the property dropped from $425,000 to $175,000 in less than 30 minutes! Needless to say, Pastor Creamer was overwhelmed, elated and very, very grateful to God. God had rewarded her obedience to leave their former church. Her decision and subsequent preparations to leave had won for her miraculous favor from God's own hand! Once again, she acted in total faith because she knew they only had about $50,000 in the bank at that time. But Pastor Creamer learned an extremely important lesson about God: When God speaks, you don't question, you just do it!

God spoke, Pastor listened, and acted in faith. They proceeded with the purchase of the 18,000 square foot warehouse. This amazing journey of faith was continuing to unfold one miracle at a time. Now, thank God, she would have a place to lead her flock. Thanks to the God of Abraham and Moses, they would not have to wander around with nowhere to go. Their Exodus March would end at this new miracle of God: his place of provision and blessing and peace. God had chosen Creamer to be the new pastor, and He had also chosen where she would go. And at the exact right time according to God's holy clock, Pastor led her faithful followers away from their proverbial Egypt to a bigger and more spacious place of praise. A place of their own by God's own design. He chose it and ordained it, and it would soon be their new church home.

The Cathedral

But what would she call her new place of praise? She began to pray and ask God for the name of the new ministry she would pastor. Prayer was the hallmark of the faith that she had. Her whole life had been built on the foundation of prayer, her new ministry was no exception. We began meeting for prayer every Monday night at 7 p.m. in the truck warehouse. Monday Night Prayer became a distinguishing characteristic of Pastor Creamer's growing ministry. One day as she walked into the white dining room of her well-kept apartment, the Spirit of God spoke these words clearly in her heart: *"The Cathedral of Fresh Fire."* That was the name God gave her for her ministry! The Cathedral of Fresh Fire, where Pentecostal flames are always burning! The new ministry now had a name, a new tagline, and a new home. Our God is an awesome God!

Exodus – Exit Us!

On the day of the Exodus March, the crowd gathered on a Sunday morning in July of 1994. I was there, too, and remember that happy day very well. Someone had prepared a large red banner with the words: *"The Cathedral of Fresh Fire"* emblazoned on the front. Those walking in front would carry the huge banner. Everyone wore something red for the occasion – a hat, or shoes, a dress, a suit, a shirt, or belt, a handbag or handkerchief. We were all united in one purpose, and our uniformity was an outward sign of the inward change that would now be clearly evident for all to see. There was a joyous atmosphere of jubilation and celebration among the group that gathered outside of the former place of worship. We were excited to be leaving our proverbial Egypt experience and to be headed toward our promised land.

Pastor Creamer walked in front with those carrying the banner. She was glowing, smiling, joyful, victorious, tall, and totally triumphant! We sang songs of victory out loud as we walked and made our way to the place where God had led. What an experience – leaving the wilderness and heading to the promised land! We had a wonderful time that day. Singing and marching through those streets was an exciting and unforgettable experience. The physical movement as we marched seemed to heighten our sense of joy as we got further and further away from the old building. We were forgetting those things behind and pressing forward to the new things ahead. We sang the songs of Zion with praise and thanksgiving, declaring the wonderful works of God as we marched through Wilmington's east side neighborhood. The neighbors watched and wondered and waved as we passed. What an unforgettable day of rejoicing it was as we marched that 1.2-mile trek triumphantly and victoriously to our happy destination!

At that time, our destination looked exactly like what it had been: a warehouse where trucks had parked and left layers upon layers of grease and grime over many years. The building would require extensive renovations to become what God intended. But through the eyes of God and through Pastor Creamer's eyes of faith on this hot morning in July of 1994, we were marching to a beautiful, spacious, cathedral with a cedar-beamed sanctuary.

When we arrived at the new building, we gathered in the large open space that would eventually become the sanctuary and, though, it was quite dirty, we all bowed in worship, in prayer, and in heartfelt, tear-stained thanks to the awesome God who'd done these miracles. We had a place to worship and a new place to praise. Pastor now had a place of her own that no one could put her out of or stop her from proclaiming God's word or from singing God's praises. On that glorious and unforgettable day, no one could praise God enough!

Yes, there was a great deal of work yet to be done, but empowered by God's miracle and led by our praising Pastor, the people would now get the work done and they would do it together. The enemy was defeated, God was exalted, and we had the victory in our new place. It was now time for Pastor Creamer and her members to do what Rev. Rainey had taught them so many times before. It was time to rise above the visible and see God, to mount up with the wings of eagles, to run and not be weary, to walk and not faint. Like Nehemiah and the Israelites preparing to rebuild the walls of Jerusalem, now the people had a mind to work.

Many Hands Make Light Work

We all worked very hard to raise the $175,000. There were chickens to clean and fry, potatoes to slice and dice, and countless dinners to sell, but the flames of our faith had been fanned by God's miracles of deliverance. We knew that with God nothing would be impossible for us now. We were about to undertake the arduous task of renovating the grimy 18,000 square foot truck warehouse into a beamed-ceiling beauty of a cathedral with a grand and glorious sanctuary. The plans also called for spacious offices, two expansive fellowship halls (one of which would be named in honor of Rev. Ross B. Rainey), new bathrooms, etc. A major battle had been fought and a resounding victory had been won, and now by the amazing, unfailing grace of her faithful God, for Pastor Creamer and her members, redemption was finally drawing nigh.

Thanks to the tireless efforts of her very committed ministry, we were able to raise the money needed to purchase the building. The building renovations required that we obtain a bank loan, so the trustees, led by the late Dr. L. Ramona Howard, rolled up their sleeves and frequently stayed up all night to finalize the process of obtaining the financing for the building renovations. Pastor Creamer is famous for saying, "Many hands make light work," and there were numerous other key players at that time who helped to get the new ministry up and running. God provided the funds to purchase the building and the financing for the renovation through the tireless efforts of faithful people. Our ability to work together confirmed the truth in another one of Pastor's favorite sayings: "Where there is unity, there is strength. Where there is strength, there is power. Where there is power, there is change." An unmistakable change was beginning to take place within the former trucking warehouse. Bishop J. Delano Ellis, the founding prelate of the Pentecostal Churches of Christ, and a father in the faith prophesied to then Evangelist Creamer before Rev. Rainey died. Bishop Ellis told her, "if a cathedral is going to be built, she would have to do it!" Bishop Ellis' words were now being fulfilled, and Pastor Creamer began building the cathedral that Rev. Rainey had envisioned a long time ago.

Restore, Refresh, Renew

Enter the bricklayers, concrete workers, plumbers, carpenters, and electricians and let the renovation and restoration begin! The project would take approximately two years. While the building was undergoing renovations, Pastor Creamer presided over the administration of the organization. Her followers were extremely faithful, gifted, and devoted believers who put their gifts and talents to work tirelessly. There were deacons who sang, praise singers who cooked, elders who were trustees, and the late Dr. L. Ramona Howard was the organist as well as the chairperson of the trustee board simultaneously. These saints were outstanding workers joyfully building a ministry where "Pentecostal flames are always burning," and everyone was happy to wear two or more hats to help build their church. The ministry and members went to their day jobs, and then came after work to assist with the church renovations. The building was being transformed much like new converts to Christ: from the inside out. Old things were passing away (or in some cases being hauled away), and all things inside were becoming new.

Renovation is a difficult process to say the least. It's dirty and dusty. It requires studying the plans and following the plans. There are ladders and wires and jackhammers and joists. There's noise and lots of different people: contractors and electricians, plumbers and carpenters, painters and more. Several walls were knocked down, floors were stripped, offices were built, bathrooms were installed. A state of the art kitchen, a large suite including office and dressing room for the Pastor, an expansive fellowship hall in honor of Reverend Rainey – it was all coming together steadily and surely. The building was being transformed from a dirty trucking warehouse into a miraculously magnificent cathedral of praise.

The sprawling sanctuary was being transformed into a space of immense beauty from the original beams in the breathtaking cedar ceiling to the colorfully decorative stained glass windows – this room was becoming the most beautiful of all. A miracle was in the making during those two years, and somehow God was helping them through it all. As the late Dr. L. Ramona Howard (chairperson of the trustee board) exclaimed one day: "church restoration has finally come!"

The Cathedral of Fresh Fire Sanctuary
"In His Honor and For His Glory"

Edg-moor Than a Community Center!

During that time, Pastor Creamer and her growing membership were forced to conduct worship services in two different locations before the renovation project was completed in 1997. We met for a time at the Edgmoor Community Center where chairs had to be set up and then taken down before and after every single service. This was a light affliction to us, and the extra work did not really bother us at all. One of the deacons, the late Voshell Lowery, was jokingly referred to as "the chairman of the chairs." We were all very grateful for the open door, so we continued to praise God fervently and faithfully while we were there. The membership and the ministry were growing, and the mothers', deacons', and trustee boards were serving actively and faithfully. Members worked together volunteering to serve as nurses or ushers, happy to do whatever their hands found to do. We had worship services and Bible studies at the center along with special services such as plays and annual days as well. It was a beautiful era in the development of the ministry, and we were all so excited about our freedom in Christ that we hardly even noticed the very humble surroundings at the community center. We were having a high time in the Lord every week, and the joy that we shared was gloriously contagious. Though not quite home yet, we were still happy in Jesus and our gratitude showed.

Helped by Harriet Tubman

It seemed to be in God's plan for the ministry to worship at a different location before the renovations were completed on the new church, so God opened another door for us at the Harriet Tubman United Methodist Church in Wilmington. Pastor Creamer continued to preach and teach at Tubman making a special sacrifice by scheduling her services at 8 a.m. on Sunday mornings so they would not interfere with the regularly scheduled services at Tubman. The Tubman church is closer to the new building than the Edgmoor Community Center, so this new open door showed us how God was moving us closer to our destination and improving our experience of Him one faithful step at a time.

At times like these we learn to follow God step by step. We can't see very far down the road, so we learn to rely on God to lead us along safely. And God does exactly that. He leads surely and safely. As we follow Him faithfully, He gradually reveals His plan. We can't see the next step until we take this step. God won't be rushed, yet His timing is perfect. He has a plan and it's up to us to follow His plan if we want the victory, the joy, the success that God brings. It's God's plan and He knows if we need to meet at a community center first, someone else's church second, and our own building last. He knows, and we do not. Our job is to follow obediently, faithfully, and triumphantly. We win when we obey Him, trust Him, and wait on Him. Pastor Creamer and her new ministry provide a powerful example for us here. "Prayer is the key," Pastor declares, "and faith unlocks the door." So we continued to pray in faith, praise with thanks, and work on the renovation of the building. We waited in faith on the timing of

God. He may not come when you want Him, but He is always right on time.

A Grand Celebration Welcomes Us Home

The day finally arrived when the newly restored facility was complete and on April 13, 1997 the glorious dedication service marked the official opening of the Cathedral of Fresh Fire, Inc. at 2300 Northeast Boulevard in Wilmington, Delaware. The extensive two-year renovation process was finally complete, and the beautiful 18,000 square foot state-of-the-art facility with a 600-seat sanctuary opened its doors for worship services in God's honor and for His glory.

Pastor Creamer, the Chief Celebrant at the dedication service, welcomed local dignitaries, political representatives, and a college of distinguished bishops presided. It was a high and holy occasion with meticulous attention given to every detail involved in dedicating our new building and ourselves to the service of God. From the Holy Spirit to the holy attire, God placed His stamp of approval, His anointing, and His blessing on the event and on the people who came to celebrate the awesome triumph for this woman of faith. Each window and door of the sprawling facility was anointed and dedicated to the service of the Lord. Various members of the clergy offered prayers, as the local community celebrated this most glorious event with Pastor Creamer, her ministry, and members.

She had believed God's promises and put her faith in Him. Though sometimes what she experienced was painfully difficult and impossibly hard, she had trusted God until He came through for them. She had faithfully endured the lawsuit, the Exodusstyle departure, and the wilderness experience while the old truck warehouse was undergoing renovation. On the day of the church dedication in April of 1997, we entered victoriously and triumphantly into the exquisitely refinished sanctuary with its 30-foot-high beamed ceilings and conducted a dedication service as unto the Lord. It was in His honor and all for His glory that bishops and dignitaries spoke and prayed and dedicated the new building to God and the fulfillment of His holy will. Her familiar saying, "you better see this thing," became the watchword of her ministry and their road map on this exciting journey of faith. She wanted them to see God and what He was doing and be thankful unto Him and bless His holy name.

After the church dedication, there was so much more to praise God for: the beautiful sanctuary with the beamed ceiling, the Ross B. Rainey Fellowship Hall, the Pastor's executive suite, the theater quality sound system, all of the various offices, and the free parking lot just to name a few. The ministry had become renown for how we praised God, and people were attracted to worship services at the Cathedral of Fresh Fire because of our ability to praise God in an unprecedented way. The hallmark of our ministry was captured in a song we sang often during their times of high praise. Frequently led by Elder Tammy Lindsay, we would sing this song until we could feel God inhabiting the praises of His people:

♫ *If you don't praise Him, well then, I'll praise Him.*
If you don't praise Him, well then, I'll praise Him.
If you don't praise Him, well then, I'll praise Him.
If you don't praise Him, well then, I'll praise Him.
For all He's done for me, yeaaa
For all He's done for me, yeaaa
For all He's done for me
What He's done for me
Watch me praise Him
Watch me praise Him
Watch me praise Him
Watch me praise Him
For all He's done for me, yeaaa
For all He's done for me, yeaaa
For all He's done for me, yeaaa
What He's done for me.

Pastor had become a master at leading her gifted praise team in songs until God's anointing touched their voices and stirred the congregation to abandon themselves in the praises of God. She would direct them to sing, and they sang as hard as they could. Some of her original praise team included Geri Nolan, Carolyn Martin, Toni Reason, Bonnie Stickney, Daylynn Drummond, and Sharlane Cormier. Others joined her team from time to time, but with the late Dr. Howard on the organ and Tammy Lindsay on the drums, Pastor Creamer would not stop until she felt God was pleased. Pastor and her praise team were textbook examples of what praise and worship is all about.

Pastor was teaching the lesson of following on to know God and the importance of staying on the pathway to eternal life in Christ. She exhorted her hearers to refuse to allow the vicissitudes of life to keep us from rising up to where God is and where He wants us to be. She admonished us to give God excellence – nothing less would suffice. Listeners were being inspired and enlivened by the anointing she has earned through day-to-day practice of faith in God's word. Her messages had gone to another level in Him, and even the squeal she would often release at the height of her sermons would permeate through the sanctuary and touch every heart in the room. Some of her most inspiring messages include "Look at the Birds" based on Matthew 6:24-33, "The Giants Keep Coming" based on I Samuel 17:32-51, and "Making It On Broken Pieces" based on Acts 27:31-44. Appendix B contains a more extensive list of her inspirational sermons that have encouraged so many with the gospel of hope and salvation in Christ.

Pastor Creamer is a woman of excellence who always has believed in and taught how important it is to give God excellence in all that we do. She is a proponent of maintaining order in God's house and leads the worship experience based on a planned, printed program that provides order and sequence (subject to change by the Holy Spirit, of course). There has always been a unique balance in Pastor Creamer's ministry between offering God ultimate praise during worship services and maintaining an order and a flow with which God can still be glorified.

To illustrate this point, notice the description below of a typical worship experience at the Cathedral of Fresh Fire that occurred during a Sunday morning service sometime in 1999 about two years after we moved into the renovated building. I was serving as Pastor Creamer's chief adjutant, so I was standing in the pulpit area in front of the choir seats at the time. Pastor was exhorting and leading the praise singers, musicians, and congregation in a particularly pervasive moment of intense praise. The following describes what happened during our time of praise:

> Several choir members were visibly overcome. Suddenly one young sister started jumping in the middle of the choir stand, knocking over a few chairs. Two nearby choir members grabbed her and held onto her the best that they could. I moved chairs out of the way to make room for the choir members to express their praise unto God. The noise level was high, and all over the sanctuary there was praising and crying; shouting, and dancing. One or two saints were running.
>
> Some of the deacons and ministry assisted, but many of the church officials were overcome themselves in this extremely pervasive and gripping moment of praise, worship, and thanksgiving to God. The people came to church that day bringing a sacrifice of praise, and Pastor Creamer kept telling the crowd how good God is, how faithful He is, how merciful He is, and how worthy of praise He is.
>
> Pastor Creamer prompted them to praise God, and they responded with exactly that: praise that spilled out into the hallway outside the sanctuary, praise that was heard throughout the building, people fanning others, nurses passing out tissues; everyone was overcome with praise.

Any who were not overcome by the atmosphere of high praise were helping to comfort those who were literally consumed emotionally with the high praises of God. It felt wonderful to be there and to see Pastor Creamer lead the people into probably the greatest moment of praise they had ever experienced. She really seemed to be praising God herself as she alternated between singing and exhorting.

Pastor Creamer directed the musicians and the praise team. They sang: "Yes, Lord, yes Lord, yes Lord, yes Lord" so rhythmically, repeatedly, and harmoniously that God Himself seemed to be enjoying this moment. It was indeed a truly beautiful moment and one that would be repeated hundreds of times in that sanctuary. Pastor Creamer was doing what she did best – leading her people straight to the heart of God. That's the place where she felt the most comfortable, the most herself, the most victorious – right near the heart and the heartbeat of God who is always worth loving, worth honoring, worth adoring, and worth praising.

The Cathedral sanctuary is an anointed place and a haven for praise, a gathering place for worship, a true get-together for God. No one who comes seeking after God will leave disappointed. God shows up by His Spirit time and time again. Pastor Creamer teaches her people about the God of salvation, the Christ of the cross, and the fresh wind of the Holy Spirit. We are learning how to be true worshippers that worship God in spirit and in truth.

Throughout the years, Pastor Creamer has gotten better and

better at leading the way toward God. She directs traffic, so to speak, encouraging and signaling those who enter to come this way toward the Holy of holies or go that way moving away from the sinfulness of the world. Her efforts to lead the people to the throne of grace have been fruitful and rewarding. She does it with absolute aplomb—masterfully, skillfully, and seemingly effortlessly. She stands tall and firm in her deep love for God and her desire to lead others to Him.

Learning to praise God and loving to worship Him are learned behaviors that must be taught and demonstrated. Someone must model the expected behavior; someone must lead the way. Someone must point us in the proper direction; someone who understands must provide a signal – one that is well timed, precise, and unmistakably clear. God has chosen pastors to carry out this task.

We'll never be able to praise or thank God enough for the open door He gave Pastor Creamer. The large gold cross up front prompts us to praise Him as we first enter into the sanctuary, and the large gold letters in the back as you are leaving encourage you to keep on praising Him until you return. The last thing you see as you exit the sanctuary are these words: *"IN HIS HONOR AND FOR HIS GLORY!"*

The Cathedral of Fresh Fire

"Where Pentecostal flames are always burning!"

Reverend Emma L. Creamer, Pastor and Founder

2300 Northeast Boulevard Wilmington, DE 19802

302-764-3344 302-764-2177 fax cathedraloffreshfire.com

Sundays at 10 a.m. Mondays at 7 p.m.

Every 1ˢᵗ Sunday, Holy Communion

Every 2d Sunday, Men's Sunday

Every 3d Sunday, Youth Sunday

Every 5ᵗʰ Sunday, Women's Sunday

Special 5 p.m. Sunday Services as Announced

LIFE LESSON 5
God Opens Doors That No Man Can Shut

Sometimes we try to force our way and push doors open in areas of our lives where doors were closed to us, but God is the one who opens doors that no man can shut and shuts doors that no man can open. We must learn to do our part, obey God's word, and then wait for Him to open the doors to us that He wants opened in our lives. Many times when one door closes to us, another opens, and we are challenged to see the open door opportunities and take advantage of them. The point is to allow God alone to control the direction of our lives and have the faith and courage to walk through the doors He opens up for us.

An effectual door open for us is one that God wants us to go through in spite of adversaries, in spite of opposition, and in spite of how much the opportunity challenges us to work hard. Never miss a God-given opportunity to make progress in God. Progress, not perfection, leads to promotion.

CHAPTER 6

AFTER GOD'S OWN HEART

✝

Pastor Creamer had asked God to give her the heart of a pastor, and He did. He gave her an unusual love for the sheep, and when they behaved like sheep do at times, she would just lovingly say: *"The People!"*

"...And I will give you pastors according to mine heart, which shall feed you with knowledge and understanding."
Jeremiah 3:15

Pastors after God's own heart are pastors who have God's heart, hear His heart, and stay in tune with His heart. Their hearts are knit together with God's heart, and they are inextricably joined at the heart with God's pure and powerful plan for His people. Pastors after God's own heart want the very best for those He has entrusted to their care. They are givers just like God, and they have hearts of gold toward God's people. These pastors would literally lay down their lives for their sheep, and many have done so figuratively speaking. Pastor Creamer is among this precious group. When she first became a pastor, she prayed and asked God to give her a pastor's heart. God answered her prayer and gave her a unique and special love and concern for her flock that she sometimes lovingly refers to as "the people!"

From His kind, loving, generous, and Fatherly heart, God has graciously given the precious gift of pastors. God has a giving heart because His very nature is generous, caring, kind, loving, and forgiving. He cares for us and wants the very best for us. His will is that none should perish, but that all should come to repentance so we can be in right relationship with Him. God is a Father who provides and protects His children. From God's heart of love and compassion, He has created pastors to care for, feed, and protect His people who are the sheep of His pasture.

A pastor after God's own heart is hard to describe with ordinary words because they are such extraordinary people. They love their people, and their people love them. These pastors want what God wants for the sheep. God is pleased with pastors who have His heart because He is highly protective of His people and will not entrust His sheep to a "wolf in sheep's clothing." To have God's heart is a necessary requisite to be an able pastor. Pastors cannot be effective unless they really do have a heart like Christ's who said, *"I am the good shepherd: the good shepherd giveth his life for the sheep."* John 10:12

It is virtually impossible to quantify the service that a pastor provides over many years. But as we examine the sacrifices Pastor Creamer has made to care for her flock, we see the tremendous sacrifice of a pastor's love. The prayers alone that she has prayed for her flock would probably exhaust our imaginations. How many prayers has this pastor prayed for her members every day and night, interceding for their needs and crying out on their behalf? From fervent prayers during Monday Night Prayer service to countless faithful prayers at members' bedsides, Pastor Creamer prays for her people continually wherever they are.

How do you add up all that Pastor has done for those entrusted to her care? As a preaching pastor, she has spent long hours of study so she can preach and teach the word of God with clarity, authority, power, and demonstration. She has preached God's word over and over again in hundreds of sermons over the years — delivering the gospel of truth after long hours of labor in the word and doctrine. The time she has spent in studying the word and delivering God's message probably totals thousands of hours. She will tell you, though, that it was time well spent in productive pursuit of the truth in God's word that will set His people free. We have to use words like "countless" and "innumerable" to describe the time and effort Pastor has spent preparing and presenting the gospel of Jesus Christ. In an effort to commemorate the many life-changing sermons Pastor has preached, Appendix B provides a chronology of some of her most historic and inspiring sermons.

Furthermore, Pastor Creamer has a heart for reaching out to those who are sick, shut-in, and cannot come to church. For that reason, she has visited virtually every hospital and most of the nursing homes in Wilmington and the surrounding area. She has always gone out of her way to show her love and concern in this way, and I have seen her travel many miles to visit and pray for a member of her ministry. To this day, Pastor still schedules regular visits to the sick to offer her heartfelt prayers in person for the people God gave to her. Her policy is to remain available and accessible to her people whenever they need her.

In addition, Pastor Creamer's ministry has frequently been characterized as one that is particularly sensitive to the needs of hurting women. Many women who have become divorced or widowed or who are single parents have found comfort and care under her pastorate. Something about Pastor Creamer's experience has brought an air and attitude that her church is a safe haven for women who have been hurt by trying circumstances in their lives. While it is not a ministry that is exclusive to hurting women only, it is one where they have found solace, strength, healing, and help for their lives.

Challenges of Female Pastors

Yet fulfilling the responsibilities of a pastor is frequently as challenging as it is rewarding. Also, female pastors face a different kind of challenge just by nature of their gender. The naturally nurturing characteristic women possess makes them more vulnerable, and people seem to be less willing to comply with female pastors and leaders.

An additional challenge for pastors is that people want the pastor's friendship, fellowship, approval, and encouragement but may not welcome the pastor's rod of correction that pulls them back into place when they've gone astray or gotten out of line. All the sheep love the smile of the pastor, the hand of the pastor, the loving message of the pastor. Yet, the same sheep may not want to hear the words of the pastor that challenge them to change, to turn, repent, and go a different way. They may resent or ignore the correction the pastor may bring. And since the heart of a pastor is to welcome all to the fold, a pastor may find among their flock some who are resistant to change or slow to obey. Bishop Audrey Bronson, long-time colleague, mentor, and friend to Pastor Creamer, has said, "If God didn't call you to pastor, the devil fooled you up on a hard job!"

The people are sometimes very dependable, but at other times very unreliable. The people! They are sometimes completely lovable and at other times, just the opposite. The people! Church members can sometimes be your biggest supporters, and at other times, they're your worst critics. They may work tirelessly on one occasion and on another, not participate at all. A pastor needs a patient heart for his or her members, and he or she must show the fruit of the Spirit – especially temperance and patience.

When many different people come together for any cause, the sum total of the gathering includes a myriad of personalities. Everyone has a history and something he or she is being healed or delivered from. People don't come to church because their lives are perfect – they come for help with their problems and issues. It has been said that the church is a hospital where Jesus is the chief of staff, the Holy Spirit is the chief administrator, and the pastor is the head of human resources! According to Jesus, *"They that are whole need not a physician: but they that are sick. I came not to call the righteous, but sinners to repentance."* Luke 5:31-32. Christians and church members are not perfect – they are just forgiven. And pastors with God's heart understand that so they just help the sheep along patiently and love them unconditionally though this sometimes takes its toll on pastors.

Pastors have the added challenge of demonstrating how to become more Christlike and showing their flock how to take up a cross daily and follow Him. This is a great responsibility and demands that a pastor have the mind of Christ and allows him or herself to be conformed to the image of Christ. I, personally, have a great deal of respect for all pastors, especially Pastor Creamer. They have to lay down their lives for the sheep but will also be tested by the occasional straying sheep. They have to speak the truth in love and restore a brother overtaken in a fault. Their calling demands that they preach the word in season and out of season and that they reprove and rebuke with all long suffering. Pastors must remain faithful to Psalm 1, without compromising their stand for the cause of Christ. What an assignment and a high calling to be called to such an awesome and difficult task!

The Pastor's Aid "Committee"

Thank God that pastors have a perfect model and example in our Lord Jesus Christ. Their help must remain in Him and Him alone. He is a "committee" of one! Jesus' humble acceptance of His fate and the meekness Jesus showed account for the power of the cross. His humility overcame hatred. His obedience overpowered rebellion. His suffering erased sin and shame. And His blood bought our redemption from eternal death, hell, and destruction. Dying, Jesus destroyed our death, and rising He restored our lives. A conquering Savior and a soon-coming King is who Jesus is and He proved it by laying down His life willingly. The cross couldn't kill Jesus and the grave couldn't hold Him. By His own admission, He could have summoned twelve legions of angels to rescue Him from the cross. Instead, just like a sheep before her shearers is dumb, He answered not His accusers and did not open up His mouth. He allowed His body to be killed so that we who put our faith in Him could gain access to eternal life. Jesus' humility exalted Him, so that now, there is no name higher than His. Jesus' obedience elevated Him. Jesus' love and compassion resurrected Him.

Likewise, the same principle applies for pastors after God's own heart like Pastor Creamer. God's heart is to overcome evil with good and to destroy darkness with light. God's heart is tender and gracious. So must ours be. So is Pastor Creamer's. God's heart is full of mercy and kindness. So must ours be. So is this Pastor's. God's heart is filled with love and graciousness. So must ours be. So is our Pastor's. No, she is not a perfect woman. Yes, she has her faults as we all do. Pastor will tell you herself that when she was new and inexperienced at pastoring, she made some mistakes. Those who know her well will also attest to the fact that she is quite strong-willed, which is not uncommon for a woman in a leadership role. But just as King David was a man after God's own heart with all of his faults and failures, so is Pastor Creamer a woman after God's own heart because she loves God with all of *her* heart. Though man looks on the outside, God looks at the heart. Pastors are human. Let's remember that and treat them accordingly. They are not Jesus, but they are His ambassadors and His representatives in the earth. Thank God that through their humanity, we ourselves can move closer to the heart of God and closer to having hearts like His.

The commendations and proclamations from many dignitaries over the years testify of her excellence in leadership and fervent love and concern for people. Vice President Joe Biden, Senator Ted Kaufman, Governor Jack Markell, and Mayor James Baker are among the many who have commended Pastor Creamer for outstanding citizenship and remarkable leadership. The pastoral robes she had to grow into many years ago have come to fit her perfectly now. After Pastor Creamer was ordained as pastor, some of the people continued to refer to her as Evangelist Creamer for awhile. One day her faithful friend, the late Dr. L. Ramona Howard, spoke up and told them: "You have to call her Pastor now!"

Pastor Emma L. Creamer
"You have to call her *Pastor* now!"

LIFE LESSON 6
Follow Me As I Follow Christ

A pastor is an awesome gift from God, and pastors are needed to help lead sheep into safety and protection. The gift of a pastor who has the heart of God and who lays down his or her life for the sheep is an immeasurable blessing and a priceless pearl. A pastor after God's own heart is an individual who loves the sheep, cares for the sheep, feeds the sheep, guides the sheep, protects the sheep, and directs the sheep in the way God would have them to go.

And God is very pleased with His pastors who have a heart like His: a heart of love, compassion, mercy, and truth. Help them however you can, for they watch for men's souls. We are called to follow them as they follow Christ. Holding their arms up achieves the victory for us all. Pray and stand in intercession for them in steadfast faith and with confidant expectation. Whatever your hands find to do to help the pastor, do it with all of your might. Work in concert with them never in contrary fashion against.

You may not understand the decision of the pastor. Neither do the sheep understand the curvature of the shepherd's staff. What we do understand is that each member has a specified purpose by divine design. There are many members yet only one body of Christ. God's will is that none should perish, but that all of us come to repentance. God's purpose is the perfecting of the saints, the work of the ministry, and the edifying of the body of Christ. He wants us all to come into the perfect man, to the measure of the stature of the fullness of Christ. So He gave us pastors.

CHAPTER 7

A POWERFUL LEGACY OF LEADERSHIP AND SERVICE

✝

Familiar with God's voice after many years in ministry, Pastor Creamer knew it was God when He impressed this message on her heart: *"This is a church of leaders."*

"Therefore seeing we have this ministry,
as we have received mercy, we faint not;"
II Corinthians 4:2

The Order of Service

By now you know that the most unforgettable and distinguishing feature of Pastor Creamer's ministry over the years has been the level of uninhibited praise and worship that can be experienced at her services. Her ministry cut its teeth on the high praises of God, which is the reason people are continually drawn to worship at the Cathedral. The word got out in the early days of the ministry that you can praise God at the Cathedral and that praise is a top priority there because Pastor and her people believe that God is worthy of His praise and that He inhabits the praises of His people. God's praises are of paramount importance in this ministry and at virtually every gathering, quality time is devoted to giving God His praise and His due glory. In fact, one of the hallmark hymns during their call to worship is: <u>We Bring the Sacrifice of Praise</u>." It's lyrics (below) express Pastor's heart perfectly and the lesson she brings to her leaders and members that no matter how they may feel when they enter God's sanctuary, they still offer up to Him the sacrifices of thanksgiving and the sacrifices of joy.

♫ *We bring the sacrifice of praise into the house of the Lord*
And we offer up to You, the sacrifices of thanksgiving
And we offer up to You, the sacrifices of joy

God is great and greatly to be praised
Glory, glory to His name;
God is great and greatly to be praised
Bless the Lord oh my soul.

I will bow before His majesty
I will lift my hands and sing
God is great and greatly to be praised
Bless the Lord, oh my soul.

The word is preached with power on Sunday mornings and over the years, Pastor Creamer is famous for admonishing her listeners to come to Christ who can help them overcome the "vicissitudes of life." Pastor Creamer wants her ministry and members to keep their focus on the mission—the conversion of souls to Christ, so she would frequently tell them, "You better see this thing." Pastor believes in training her leaders to give God excellence in all things, and she therefore allows her associate pastors, elders, ministers, and others the opportunity to preach the word of God. Because the fresh fire of the Holy Spirit continues to burn up everything that is not like God in a person's life, the church services have always been blessed. Countless souls have given their hearts to Christ over the years of Pastor Creamer's ministry, and countless more have received the gift of the infilling of the Holy Spirit because the Pentecostal flames have never stopped burning in the Cathedral.

Holy Communion is celebrated the first Sunday morning of each month, and Pastor Creamer participates in Holy Communion every day and encourages the same for her ministry and membership. Christenings occur quarterly at the Cathedral, and the annual outdoor baptism services are always beautiful occasions graced by the presence and glory of God and His Spirit.

Leaders and members enjoy further opportunities for worship

and praise through Sunday afternoon worship services. Afternoon services are scheduled periodically throughout the year, and many of the church's auxiliaries utilize these services to be a financial blessing to the ministry.

"And straightway coming up out of the water, he saw the heavens opened, and the Spirit like a dove descending upon him." Mark 1:10

The Ministry of the Cathedral of Fresh Fire
Conclusion of the Annual Baptism Service
Sandy Cove Christian Retreat
"We lift our hands in total praise to God."

Psalms, Hymns, and Spiritual Songs

Pastor Creamer has enjoyed a successful music ministry dating back to the time when she taught herself to play on a broken piano on which only two of the keys actually worked. From singing with the legendary Dorothy Norwood and Pastor Shirley Ceasar to forming the Emma Creamer Singers, her music ministry has always had an exceptional and powerful anointing. She understands that music facilitates worship, and has worked very hard to ensure that her music is a sweet sound in God's ears. Backed up by a powerful praise team, Pastor Creamer is a master at leading a song until it really ministers to the hearts and needs of the listening congregation.

God has always blessed her to have gifted singers and musicians, along with a very talented and extremely faithful band. Today, her music ministry is led by Charles Finney, a member of the Mighty Aires national recording group. There are four choirs: The Children's Choir, The New Generation Youth Choir, The Cathedral Choir, and the Women's Choir. God has been extremely faithful to Pastor over the years of her powerful music ministry – a ministry that has carried her all the way from the piano to the pulpit. For a historical perspective of Pastor Creamer's musical accomplishments, see her Memorable Ministry of Music in Appendix D.

God Answers Monday Night Prayers

A primary reason for the success of this ministry is the continuous prayers offered to God during the weekly Monday Night Prayer service that has continued for all 22 years of Pastor Creamer's tenure as senior pastor and founder of the ministry. This is a weekly time for corporate fasting and prayer that causes the ministry to be blessed above measure. Over the years, the number is far too many to count who have received miraculous answers to prayers after being anointed in one of Pastor Creamer's Monday Night prayer lines. On a typical Monday night, Pastor would ask everyone in the sanctuary to line up in the center aisle, and she anointed each one with oil and prayed the prayer of faith for each and every person in the line. As Pastor Creamer laid hands on the people, they were frequently slain in the Spirit and received healing from a sickness, an emotional problem, a financial problem, etc. She would lay hands and pray for everyone, including those in her ministry.

There is something amazing about these prayer meetings on Monday nights. We always leave feeling uplifted and blessed, and there are many testimonies of physical healings, financial miracles, and other answers to prayers. I have observed over many years that those who have committed themselves to attend Monday night prayer regularly gain wholeness in their lives after a sustained period of faithfulness to these services. I believe this is God's response to the amount of sacrifice that is required to attend service on a Monday night when most others are resting after Sunday's busy schedule. God always honors the sacrifice and responds to the prayers that are prayed at Monday Night

Prayer. It's a service worth attending if you are anywhere near the Wilmington area on a Monday evening at seven o'clock.

Teach, Teacher!

Members and leaders are taught the word of God through Bible studies, Sunday school, and Bible readings each week. Sunday school classes are held weekly for all ages, and those attending receive instruction based on an approved curriculum of biblical study that aims to teach the principles behind the stories in the Bible. Weekly Bible study sessions focus on practical application of biblical principles and help members to see how to live the word of God on a daily basis. Further attention to the word of God is presented weekly during the Monday evening service. On Monday nights, the members read selected chapters from the Bible so that by the end of the year, we have read through the entire Bible.

After 22 years of pastoring and more than 46 years in Christian ministry and service, Pastor Creamer continues to "set the table" with opportunities for learning the word of God and how to apply it to our everyday lives. She's building a legacy based on sound biblical doctrine and feels so strongly about the importance of a biblical education that in 2003 her church became a charter campus affiliate of the Chesapeake Bible College & Seminary in Ridgely, Maryland. For the Cathedral, this phrase says it all about Christian education: "Thy word is all that matters!"

A Royal Priesthood

Pastor Creamer preaches and teaches for the purpose of revolutionizing one's character, and preparing and equipping her members to eventually be ready to use their gifts in ministry leadership and service. She emphasizes the point that in order to become a good leader, you must first be a good follower. She also teaches her leaders that "if nobody is following you, you're just a man taking a walk." Leadership training has included formal workshops, seminars, and meetings, as well as learning "on the floor." Her ministry leaders learned to stay alert, to watch her, and stay prepared to be called on to minister at any time. It's not unusual to hear her daughter, Co-Pastor Elect Helena Creamer, encouraging us to "Let the Lord use you!" In addition, Pastor Creamer has never tolerated slothfulness in leaders and could often be heard admonishing us to "move quickly!" Punctuality is a priority for her, and she teaches that "if you can be on time for your job on Monday, you can be on time for God on Sunday." Her guiding principle in developing strong leaders is to always give God excellence in all that you do.

When her ministry was birthed, God told Pastor Creamer that she had a "church of leaders." Most who join and remain members are being trained for some aspect of Christian ministry and leadership. Pastor Creamer has mentored many over the years and has ordained pastors, elders, evangelists, ministers, deacons, and missionaries into Christian ministry and service. These are exceptional saints who have accepted the call of sacrifice and service to spend their lives for the gospel of Christ. They provide faithful service week after week and in many ways are like the pillars of their church. Many continue to serve with her faithfully at the Cathedral, while others have moved on to start their own ministries and churches in different locations throughout the U.S. Although she humbly refuses the title, Pastor Creamer actually walks in the office of a bishop. To God be the glory for a "church full of leaders."

Servant Leaders

God has also blessed Pastor with a committed and especially hard-working lay ministry including the trustees' board, mothers' board, musicians, ushers, nurses, security team, culinary staff, and cleaning staff. Many of them fulfill more than one assignment at the Cathedral and wear two or more "hats" of responsibility. These saints are sweetly saved by Jesus, and their level of service shows it. God has favored Pastor Creamer with people who have sold out to Christ as she sold out to Christ and who use their gifts and talents to bring glory to God.

Other active and faithful ministries at the Cathedral include the men's, women's, and new members' ministries; the youth, and dance ministries; and the outreach, health/wellness, and Pastor's support ministries. The many contributions of these leaders, their sacrifices, and their service have been instrumental in making the Cathedral a strong witness to the power of God in operation in the believer's life. "Many hands make light work," says Pastor Creamer, and whatever their hands find to do, these saints do it with all of their might. A listing of her current ministry departments is shown in Appendix F.

Young Men Dream Dreams

Pastor Creamer has built an exceptional youth ministry over the years because of her firm commitment to working for the salvation of young people. Most of the young people were not permitted to do very much in church when she was growing up. For that reason, she has taken the opposite approach in her own ministry and has developed a youth ministry so strong that it is called the "Youth Church" and has a Youth Pastor. Every third Sunday is devoted to the development of young people at the Cathedral, and those youth who are aspiring to leadership roles in ministry have the opportunity to actively participate in leading the service. The junior ministry includes junior deacons and missionaries, the New Generation Youth Choir, Danz Praiz, the Children's Church, and the Children's Choir, and they all are vitally important in the life and activities of the Cathedral of Fresh Fire. In addition, Pastor Creamer founded the very first liturgical dancers in the state of Delaware. The original dancers were Tabita Ares, Lanisha Larkin, and Tierney Spencer, and they set the precedent and the standard of excellence for praise dancers today. The dancers, now known as Danz Praiz, have ministered in liturgical dance to rave reviews in churches, theaters, and at various city, county, and state events.

Danz Praiz
"Praise him with the timbrel and praise him with the dance"

Back Row L to R Tabita Ares, Destiny Yancey, Tiffany Johnson, Shantell Wooten, Pastor Creamer, Amber Clay, Simone Blackshear, Sharniece Smith, Shanice Oree, Arielle Clay, Deborah Turner

Back Right L to R Monique Yancey, Londrea Gordon, Andrea Torres Glover

Front Row L to R Tn'nia Fortson, Rahjae King, Brenae Brown, Jazmine Harris

I Once Was Young

The New Generation Youth Choir ministers contemporary gospel music that is relevant to teenagers, young adults, and the young-at-heart as well. For the little ones, Children's Church is offered so they can learn about God and His word in a way that is easy for them to understand. In addition, the Children's Church Choir always receives a standing ovation when their little voices are heard singing songs like this one that encourage us to hold on to our hope in God's promises. The song is entitled <u>God Put a Rainbow in the Sky.</u>

> ♫ *God put a rainbow in the sky.*
> *God put a rainbow in the sky.*
> *When it looked like the sun wouldn't shine anymore,*
> *God put a rainbow in the sky.*
> *Wait a minute, wait a minute,*
> *Looks like I see a rainbow.*
> *Way over yonder,*
> *Looks like I see a rainbow.*
> *When it looked like the sun wouldn't shine anymore,*
> *God put a rainbow in the sky.*

Pastor Creamer often says that if we don't teach, encourage, and celebrate our children, then the world and the streets will. She knows firsthand the value of getting the youth involved at a young age and has seen her diligent efforts pay off in big dividends in her popular youth ministry. The ministry continues to maintain its focus on the direct application of Proverbs 22:6 – training the young people in the way they should go so that even when they are old, they will not depart from it.

Good Stewards

Pastor Creamer has been a model of good financial stewardship as her ministry has grown over the years. She set the standard for sacrificial giving by donating her entire life savings to the ministry and living in an apartment for many years. She exemplifies the principles of faithful tithing and giving, and God has rewarded her faithfulness by meeting every ministry need. God has always blessed Pastor Creamer with committed followers who have worked tirelessly over the years conducting many successful fund raisers including church dinners, afternoon church services (called annual days), guest ministers, musicians, and choirs. Her fund raising efforts have included hosting legendary gospel artists such as Vickie Wynans and Richard Smallwood, and God has kept His promise to Pastor Creamer to "supply all of her needs."

Her ministry paid off the $400,000 mortgage loan in November 2012 that was obtained to renovate the truck warehouse into the Cathedral. Pastor's vision was for the church to pay the mortgage off early in order to save over $20,000 in interest on the loan, so she led an aggressive capital campaign fund raising effort that ultimately became an overwhelming success. The mortgage burning celebration was a grand celebration of praise and thanksgiving to God that culminated with the actual burning of the mortgage on April 21, 2013. The three-week long series of celebration services included riveting messages from such distinguished preachers as Bishop Audrey Bronson, Bishop J. Delano Ellis, II, Bishop Bruce Parham, and Rev. Silvester

Beaman among others. The mortgage burning is another amazing milestone in Pastor Creamer's life of ministry and service and is a glowing example of how to be a good steward over God's finances even during challenging economic times. We are filled with praise and thanksgiving for this miracle of God! All that is left now of that $400,000 debt is a jar filled with ashes on Pastor's bookshelf. What a mighty God we serve! Your miracle may take years of faith and works, but sooner or later, God will reduce your challenging test to a jar full of ashes, too! He did it for us, so be encouraged because He can do it for you, too! He who started the work will be faithful to complete it in you.

Going Into All the World

Street Outreach. God positioned the Cathedral of Fresh Fire in a location that has facilitated its ability to reach out to the neighboring community with the message of hope and salvation—the message of Christ. Helping people is always God's purpose and Pastor Creamer's purpose as well. The Cathedral outreach has a hands-on approach which featured a bold street outreach ministry for many years. The outreach ministry team led souls to Christ in front of local liquor stores, worked with prostitutes and drug addicts in the nearby neighborhood, and now has members from the surrounding area who've become saved and delivered. The missionaries have been instrumental in reaching out to the hurting by conducting monthly feedings, and the ministry conducts annual community baptism services, annual food drives, and various other outreach and giveaway events.

Prison Outreach. For several years, a comprehensive outreach ministry included regular visits to the local men's prison, the women's prison, a local women's shelter, and nursing homes. In addition, the ministry conducts regular visits to the sick and shut-in and remains firm in its commitment to reach out in whatever way it can to be a help to those who are sick and shut-in. The goal is practical application of Matthew 25:34-36:

"...Come, ye blessed of my Father, inherit the kingdom prepared for you from the foundation of the world: For I was an hungered, and ye gave me meat: I was thirsty, and ye gave me drink: I was a stranger, and ye took me in: Naked, and ye clothed me: I was sick, and ye visited me: I was in prison, and ye came unto me."

The Wings of Healing Telecast. Pastor Creamer's legacy of leadership was demonstrated through the years of her weekly television broadcasts called "The Wings of Healing" which showed Pastor Creamer's dynamic sermons for the local television viewing audience. The theme of the telecast was based on Malachi 4:2: *"But unto you that fear my name shall the Sun of righteousness arise with healing in his wings. . ."* The purpose of the telecast was outreach also, and her ministry is blessed enough to have a state-of-the-art sound system as well as the technicians who have the expertise to operate the system effectively.

Taking the Gospel to the Grand

Pastor Creamer's commitment to outreach is further evidenced in the fact that she produced two successful, original gospel stage plays. Both plays were written, directed, and performed by members of her ministry, and both aimed to focus the community on the life and ministry of Christ the Savior and His finished work on the cross. Each play was designed for outreach, and each became a financial blessing to the ministry as well.

The first play, entitled <u>The Blood</u>, played to a sellout audience of approximately 1,100 at the Grand Opera House in Wilmington. The playwrights (Helena Creamer, Barbara Way Washington, and Michael Way) were subsequently nominated for the Hollywood Gospel Insider Music Award for gospel playwrights in 2004 and traveled to Hollywood for the awards ceremony to be among gospel legends like Andre Crouch and Hezekiah Walker.

The ministry's second stage play production in 2008, <u>Behold the Lamb</u>, was also successful in reaching out in a creative way with the message of God's love for us through Jesus Christ who is the Lamb and our perfect sacrifice. <u>Behold the Lamb</u>, written by Helena Creamer, featured a breathtakingly moving scene depicting the resurrection of Christ that brought the house to their feet in Wilmington's Grand Opera House in 2008. These stage plays were original productions that were carried out to completion with no expense spared by Pastor Creamer. They were directed, produced, and performed at a level of excellence that met industry standards for the production of live stage plays. <u>The Blood</u> and <u>Behold the Lamb</u> illustrated conclusively Pastor Creamer's resolve and commitment to reach out to the lost regardless of the cost and to give God excellence in all that you do.

A Lasting Legacy of Faith

The most remarkable aspect of Pastor Creamer's legacy of leadership is her teaching and example of the importance of faith. Her very life has been a complete journey of faith. Although she herself is not perfect, she has shown from her childhood and throughout her lifetime walk with God a nearly perfect faith in God who is perfect in His great faithfulness to us. Her mantra has always been that prayer is the key, and faith unlocks the door. She will lead the work, but faith accomplishes the task. The kind of faith that pleases God is the kind that believes that He will do just what He said He would do in the word of God. God is pleased with faith that moves in obedience even when one does not see how God will do what He's promised. God is pleased with faith that will remain steadfast until vicious attacks become victorious triumphs for the people believing Him and standing in faith.

It is important to remember, however, that all of our faith is a gift from God. *"For by grace are ye saved through faith; and that not of ourselves; it is the gift of God: Not of works lest any man should boast."* (Ephesians 2:8) Faith is a beautiful and powerful gift. *"For I say, through the grace given unto me, to every man that is among you, not to think of himself more highly than he ought to think; but to think soberly, according as God hath dealt to every man the measure of faith."* (Romans 12:3) God gave us faith and the ability to have faith in Him, so He gets all the credit, glory, and honor for that. We take up the shield of faith because it's up to us to act on the faith God gave us. We are required to use our faith, and faith without works is still dead. Pastor Creamer is a model of faith in action because God gifted her with an extra measure of faith in Him.

Her life of faith has left an indelible mark on the lives of those Pastor Creamer has touched. Her faith in God has caused her to overcome many attacks on her health, like the time she suffered a very serious thyroid illness that caused her to lose 40 pounds in two weeks. Her eyes were extremely protruded, and the doctors told her she would never again be able to even lift a broom to sweep a floor. But her absolute faith and trust in the Lord and His power to heal sustained her, and God touched and healed her miraculously! Needless to say, she will always be grateful to God for His healing touch then and throughout the years of her life.

It takes great faith to not only lay hands on the sick and they recover but to then put those people to work in your ministry and train them to eventually become faithful ministers, leaders, and preachers of the gospel themselves. Whatever kind of faith that takes, God gave it to Pastor Creamer, and she has passed it on to her leaders and members.

Her faith has been matched with works throughout the years, but the underlying foundation and overriding theme of the success Pastor Creamer has enjoyed is one thing and one thing only: her mountain-moving faith in God who is able to do exceeding abundantly above all we can either ask or think. That faith has never changed and it never will. Her legacy of faith endures today and is evidenced in her life and ministry in so many ways. The lives she's touched over the years are all better off because they've been touched by her faith. They have heard her faith-filled sermons and been encouraged by her faithful songs. Lives have been changed by her teachings of faith, her example of faith, and her life lived by faith. The people have been able to see a living model of the kind of faith that pleases God, and they have become better and stronger because of it. Even those who did not or could not continue on with Pastor Creamer will attest to how her strong faith had a great impact on their lives. Those who have long since moved on will tell you that she is still their Pastor, her church is still their church, and her faith in God made a lasting change in them.

Faith is greater than any enemy, any obstacle, any hindrance, and any problem because God is greater. So if our faith is in God rather than in people or the problem itself, God always brings us through and brings us out. He always causes us to triumph and always causes us to win. He never goes back on His word or His promises, and He never forsakes His people. When we put our faith and trust in Him, He always comes through for us—always. When we walk by faith in God and refuse to be moved by what we see, God comes through on our behalf over and over and over again. When we refuse to doubt God, we refuse to lose. When we refuse to lay our faith in God aside, we refuse to lay our victory aside. When we keep hoping on in faith, we eventually see the end result of that faith which always equals our victory. Faith in God is the way to a victorious life. This is what Pastor Creamer learned to do so well, and she helped so many others to do the same. Pastor learned that the victory that overcomes the world and its troubles is our faith.

Over the years, Pastor has shown her members and leaders by her example exactly the kind of faith that we need:

Faith to believe for the impossible.
Faith to see the invisible.
Faith to do all things through Christ who strengthens us.
Faith to cast out demons and speak with new tongues.
Faith to build a body of Christian believers.
Faith to mold leaders and shape them in the image of Christ.
Faith to overcome opposition and spiritual wickedness.

Faith to sing God's praises in a strange land.

Faith to conquer every foe.

Faith to preach on Sunday, pray on Monday, rest on Tuesday, visit on Wednesday, teach on Thursday, do the work of an evangelist on Friday, and make full proof of thy ministry on Saturday.

By far, the greatest impact that Pastor Creamer's ministry has made is her example of unwavering, immovable, unshakeable faith in God. This is the greatest lesson of all to her followers and to those who read about her journey of faith. Believe God, love God, have faith in God, and serve God, and He will see you through. Many times over the years, we have heard Pastor exclaim with joy, "I'm so blessed I don't know what to do with myself!" She's blessed because she is a woman of faith.

Can we learn from the example of her life? Let's do it, saints. Let's turn the corner in our own personal journeys of faith. Let's step up and do more walking by faith, and not by sight. Let's not look at the things that are seen for the things that are seen are temporary. Let's focus on the things that are unseen which are eternal. Since we are living to live again and striving to make heaven our final resting place, let's set our affection on things above where Christ is seated at the right hand of God, not on things on the earth. Let's place more faith in God Elohim, the Creator and Sustainer of life. Let us trust Him and hope in Him. He has promised to never leave us and never forsake us. He will fight every battle, and give us the victory. He will heal every hurt and wipe away every tear. God will handle every one of our cares, if we cast them all on Him. He is faithful, and His faithfulness is very great.   With all that Pastor Creamer has given throughout her life of service and sacrifices for others, the most precious and priceless gift she has given is the gift of her boundless and unwavering **F-A-I-T-H**: Forsaking All I Trust Him!

LIFE LESSON 7
Serving Others Is Supreme

Every one who lives will die, and when we die we will leave some type of legacy behind based on how we lived the lives God gave us. To live a life of service and to develop future leaders is a powerful legacy to leave behind. Serving others is life's ultimate work, and training the young in the way they should go is extremely important to the success of generations to come. Christian leadership and service signifies a life well lived and is a powerful example for others to follow.

Impact the future, make a mark, and leave a legacy that the passing of time can never erase. Serve God and somebody, anybody other than yourself. Doing what? Do what humbles the heart and uplifts a life whatever that might be. To develop good leaders takes a lifetime of disciplined work and purposeful effort. The highest calling is to be a servant leader advancing the cause of Christ and spending your life in service to God and others.

According to Oswald Chambers, "Jesus Christ's idea of a New Testament saint is not one who proclaims the Gospel merely, but one who becomes broken bread and poured out wine in the hands of Jesus Christ for other lives." Among the names of great and noble men and women, I cannot think of one who was not first a servant.

CHAPTER 8

I'VE GOT TO MAKE IT

✝

Pastor Creamer often says with a twinkle in her eye, *"Where Jesus is, 'tis heaven there."*

"And the twelve gates were twelve pearls; every several gate was of one pearl: and the street of the city was pure gold, as it were transparent glass … And the city had no need of the sun … to shine in it: for the glory of God did lighten it, and the Lamb is the light thereof. And the nations of them which are saved shall walk in the light of it…"
Revelation 21:21, 23-24

Still standing tall in God after decades in ministry, Pastor Creamer will tell you that, yes, God will bless you if you have faith in Him and continue to live your life for Him. She will tell you of the many blessings that God has given her. All of the people He gave her to love and cherish: her natural family, her church family, and so many loyal friends. The spiritual blessings have been incredible too: the souls saved, the bodies healed, the lives changed over the years. The spiritual blessings alone are far too numerous to mention.

She would have to include all of the material blessings as well: the trip to Israel and the complimentary vacations to tropical islands and other exotic places around the world. She is so grateful for the many, many gifts of all kinds from friends, members, and well-wishers over the years. Yes, Pastor is grateful for the beautiful home that God gave her after so many years of apartment living. She says "Thank you, Jesus" for each and every spiritual and material blessing that God has given throughout her many years of ministry service. God is a rewarder of those who diligently seek Him, and He has given this Pastor many earthly rewards to prove the absolute integrity of His word and His promises.

Yes, God's earthly rewards to Pastor Creamer have been phenomenal. She will tell you, though, that nothing is as precious as Jesus and that she'd rather have Jesus than silver and gold. She will lift her hands with a heart of thanksgiving and a tear may glisten in her eye as she reminds you that the greatest blessing of all is to make it to where Jesus is – to the city called Heaven. Pastor is looking for her heavenly reward. This has been the purpose of her life of ministry and service, and it remains the ultimate goal of her teaching, preaching, singing, and living.

Some years ago, the Cathedral Choir would frequently sing these lyrics from Hezekiah Walker's song, Make It To That City:

> ♪ *I've got to make it. With Jesus on my side, I know I will.*
> *I've got to make it, make it to that city called Heaven.*
> *Make it to the city called Heaven.*
> *Make it to the city called Heaven.*
> *If it costs my life, I've got to make it.*
> *Make it to the city called Heaven.*
> *If it costs my life, I've got to make it.*
> *Make it to the city called Heaven.*
> *I've got to make it, make it*
> *Make it to that city.*
> *I've got to make it, make it*
> *Make it to that city.*
> *Citay, citay, citay, citay, citay, citay, citay, citay . . .*
> *I've got to make it!*

The congregation would be moved to radical praise at the thought of finally making it to heaven after the trials, tribulations, and vicissitudes of life. All else pales in comparison to the thought of heaven. It's the whole point, the only point, and nothing but the point so help us God! There's nothing more precious than Jesus, and we want to behold Him face to face. He's the reason why we sing. And the cry of our hearts remains: "I've got to make it – make it to the city called heaven."

It's the point of the salvation message of the gospel of Jesus

Christ. It's the point of a ministry like the one Pastor Creamer has. The goal is to win souls to the kingdom of heaven – for each one to reach one for salvation in Christ by telling them that *"God so loved the world that He gave His only begotten Son that whosoever believeth in Him should not perish but have everlasting life."* (John 3:16) The sum total and the entire point is everlasting life! We know from II Peter 3:9 that God's will is that none should perish, but that all should come to repentance. Our prayer is that someone would read these words and confess aloud that Jesus is their Lord and believe in their hearts that God raised Jesus from the dead, so that they can be saved. Our hope is that Pastor Creamer's ministry would impact someone who reads this work, and that man or woman or boy or girl would come running to God crying, "what must I do to be saved?"

This is what her 46 years of ministry has been all about: the salvation of men's souls. It's been for the purpose of adding souls to the kingdom of heaven. It has not been for fame or fortune or prestige or notoriety. No, Pastor Creamer is not interested in having her name known. She wants the name of Jesus known. She wants Christ proclaimed from the rooftops. She lives to lift up His name, because she believes what Jesus said in John 12:32: *"that I, if I be lifted up from the earth, I will draw all men unto Me."* That's been the only point of her life and her life's work: all men unto salvation, all men unto Himself. Because *"Neither is there salvation in any other: for there is none other name under heaven given among men whereby we must be saved."* (Acts 4:12).

With all that's she's done and all that her life has exemplified in terms of fortitude, faith, perseverance, and strength, Pastor Creamer's name cannot save men's souls. It is only by faith in the name of Jesus and in the finished work of the cross of Christ that men can be saved. It is only through belief in the power of the resurrected Christ who is now seated at the right hand of God the Father that men can be saved. It is only in making a quality decision to accept Jesus Christ as Lord of our lives. It is only in asking God to forgive our sins and take control of our lives and allowing Christ to be Lord that men can be saved. It is a quality decision each person must make within his or her own heart. And no one escapes from having to one day make a choice. Each one must decide for him or herself to accept Christ as Savior and receive Him as Lord. It's a decision between you and God. I tried Him one day and found Him to be not only a Savior but also a friend. The words of the familiar hymn, *"What A Friend We Have In Jesus,"* show us that the way of salvation is as easy as a simple prayer:

> ♫ *What a friend we have in Jesus*
> *All our sins and griefs to bear*
> *What a privilege to carry*
> *Everything to God in prayer*
> *Oh what peace we often forfeit*
> *Oh what needless pain we bear*
> *All because we do not carry*
> *Everything to God in prayer.*

The Most Important Prayer of Them All

"Everything to God in prayer" means exactly that – everything that we are and everything that we are not. Take it all to God in prayer with a surrendered heart and a simple prayer saying:

"God, please forgive me of my sins. I know that I've done wrong but I want to do right. I believe you sent your Son Jesus to die for my sins, and I believe that Jesus rose from the dead to give me eternal life. I accept Jesus Christ as my Savior, and I surrender my life to Him. Save me and cleanse me, Jesus, and take over as Lord of my life. Thank you, Jesus, for saving me today and writing my name in the Lamb's book of life. I now have eternal life through Jesus Christ, my Savior and my Lord. I believe that right now I am born again to new life in Christ. I pray this prayer willingly with my whole heart. In Jesus' name, I am saved today. Amen."

God is so wonderful and gracious and kind that this is all it takes to receive salvation and new life in Christ – one simple, heartfelt prayer spoken in a moment and in the twinkling of eye. No fanfare is necessary, and no crowds are needed. All that is needed is you and your heart and God and His ears. That's all it takes. And when you take that simple step, oh how the angels in heaven begin rejoicing because you are one more soul that is saved! If you've prayed the simple prayer above and you sincerely meant it in your heart, you are now born again and all heaven is rejoicing right this moment for your entrance into the Lamb's Book of Life and your future place that belongs to you now up in heaven. You shall have everlasting life, because you're born again!

Find A Bible-Believing Church

If you've just become born again because you've prayed the prayer above (called "The Sinner's Prayer), find a Bible-believing church to attend this coming Sunday. Tell the Pastor there that you gave your life to Christ today, and he or she will help you get started in your new life in Christ. It is important to get connected with other Christians so that you can get stronger and grow in your new life in Christ. Association brings assimilation, and we tend to act like those around us, so it's important to be around others who are also saved from their sins through faith in Jesus Christ as their Lord.

The Bible: The Best Selling Book of All Time

In addition to finding a good church, you will need a Holy Bible so that you can read what God has said in His word. In your Bible, it's good to start reading Matthew, Mark, Luke, and John because these are the books of the Bible that explain about Christ. As a new believer, it's important to learn about our Lord and Savior Jesus Christ as quickly as we can. He is the foundation of our faith and the cornerstone of what we believe. Christ gives us access to abundant life now and to eternal life in the hereafter. So Bible reading and study is necessary for every Christian—those new to the faith and those who've been in it a long time. There is no successful Christian who does not know much about God's word, for it provides God's promises to us, His provision for us, and His purpose for our lives.

Talk With God Every Day (aka Prayer)

Regular prayer is vitally important as well. Pray daily, and you will find yourself getting stronger and stronger in your relationship with God. You don't need to use fancy words when you pray to God; you just need to be humble and honest and speak from your heart. There are many types of prayers that you will learn along the way; just make some time every day to spend with God in prayer. One simple formula for prayer is known as the ACTS method of prayer:

A – Adoration (express your love for God)
C – Confession (admit your sins)
T – Thanksgiving (express thanks)
S – Supplication (request your needs and desires)

Elder Roslyn Whitehurst explains in her booklet, Pray With Purpose and Power, that there are more than 5,000 personal promises of prayer in the Bible, and she refers us to Matthew 21:22: *"And all things, whatsoever ye shall ask in prayer, believing, ye shall receive."* Remember, prayer is the key, and faith unlocks the door.

The Helpful Holy Spirit

Another important part of new life in Christ is the baptism of the Holy Spirit. Elder Carolyn Peak writes in her booklet, The Holy Spirit: An Introductory Study, that the baptism of the Holy Spirit is mentioned several times in the Bible including in Mark 1:8 which says: *"I indeed baptized you with water: but he shall baptize you with the Holy Ghost."* The Holy Spirit is also referred to as the Holy Ghost in the Bible. Once again, it's as simple as a single prayer to receive this awesome and comforting aspect of the Christian experience. Luke 11:9-13 explains how to receive the Holy Spirit and His indwelling power:

> *"And I say unto, Ask, and it shall be given you; seek, and ye shall find; knock, and it shall be opened unto you. For every one that asketh receiveth; and he that seeketh findeth; and to him that knocketh it shall be opened. If a son shall ask bread of any of you that is a father, will he give him a stone? or if he ask a fish, will he for a fish give him a serpent? Or if he shall ask an egg, will he offer him a scorpion? If ye then, being evil, know how to give good gifts unto your children: how much more shall your heavenly Father give the Holy Spirit to them that ask him?"*

At first, new believers are referred to as new babes in Christ, thus the term "born again." Then as we begin to grow and mature in God, the baptism of the Holy Spirit takes us to a new level of power, strength, and faith in Him. When I first became filled with the Holy Spirit, I just prayed a simple prayer based on my faith in what God has said in Luke 11:13 and Acts 2:4, and immediately I began to speak in my new prayer language. This is often referred to as speaking in an unknown tongue. I had already been a Christian for about three years when I received the baptism of the Holy Spirit, and, spiritually speaking, it felt as if I had just graduated from high school and gone on to college. It is a very helpful, strengthening, and vital experience for every believer to have. Many Christians also refer to this as becoming "filled with the Holy Spirit as evidenced by speaking in an unknown tongue." My own experience of becoming filled with the Holy Spirit was both peaceful and powerful, and it strengthened me as I was growing in my new life in Christ. Just pray this simple prayer if you'd like to become filled with the Holy Spirit:

> *"God, I come to you in the name of Jesus who is my Savior, my Lord. I want to be filled up with your precious Holy Spirit, and God your word says I need only to ask you to fill me and I will be filled with Your Spirit. So in complete faith I ask You to let Your precious Holy Spirit fill me right here and right now. I believe I receive my baptism in the Holy Spirit right now because I have asked in faith, Father. So I thank you right now for filling me with Your Spirit, God. In Jesus' name, I pray. Amen."*

If you prayed that prayer, you've become filled with God's precious Holy Spirit, and we are rejoicing with you today. You may contact the Cathedral of Fresh Fire (see Appendix G), and someone from the ministry can answer any questions you may have about new life in Christ Jesus. You are an important part of the family of God, and there is nothing more important than your relationship with God through Christ. In the words of one of Pastor Creamer's original songs: *"There is nothing as precious as*

Jesus; there's nothing as precious as He." Congratulations and God bless you in your new life in Christ.

Sheep Beget Sheep

And for those reading this who are already connected to God through Christ, Pastor also teaches that "sheep beget sheep." Her ministry has always been about winning souls to Christ, so let's follow her example to win the lost at any cost. Pastor's message in her initial sermon was entitled: "We Need A Reminder." And people need a reminder in these last and evil days. They need us to tell them, "You must be born again." They need to understand that God loved them so much that He gave Jesus, and they need us to remind them that sooner or later they'll need to choose Christ as Savior (or reject Him as such). People need to be reminded that their failure to make a decision *for* Christ is, by default, a decision against Him. Believers everywhere must be about our heavenly Father's business, planting the seeds of the gospel and winning souls for Christ. Now more than ever, people need the Lord. They need us to tell them what Christ told the multitudes in Matthew 13:45-50:

> *"Again, the kingdom of heaven is like unto a merchant man, seeking goodly pearls: Who, when he had found one pearl of great price, went and sold all that he had, and bought it. Again, the kingdom of heaven is like unto a net, that was cast into the sea, and gathered of every kind: Which, when it was full, they drew to shore, and sat down, and gathered the good into vessels, but cast the bad away. So shall it be at the end of the world: the angels shall come forth, and sever the wicked*

from among the just, And shall cast them into the furnace of
fire: there shall be wailing and gnashing of teeth."

We have to tell them about heaven, and we have to tell them about hell just like Jesus did in the preceding passage. We cannot sidestep the issue of hell and the fact that it is a real place referred to several places in the Bible with names like Sheol, the lake of fire, and hell. We try to avoid talking to the world about hell, but God said that *"My people are destroyed for lack of knowledge."* (Hosea 4:6) If we love them, we will tell them the truth.

We must tell them that hell was prepared for the devil and his followers—not for humans. We must help them to understand that eternity is forever and where they spend that eternity is very important. We need to help them understand that God is eternal. *"Before the mountains were brought forth, or ever thou hadst formed the earth and the world, even from everlasting to everlasting, thou art God."* (Psalm 90:2) God created man in His image and after His likeness, so He made man to exist eternally as well. We need them to know that God created us to exist with Him eternally unless we reject God and refuse what He offers. We must remind them that the part of a human that is not visible (the soul and the spirit) is more important than the part that is visible (the flesh and the body). The body will decay and die, but the soul and the spirit will live forever.

God's original intention was not to reject mankind or to punish mankind. God is loving, pure, pious, righteous, holy, peaceful, kind, gentle, gracious, generous, helpful, and virtuous. God created man for communion, friendship, and relationship with Him. God wants us to be with Him, to live for Him, to stay in relationship with Him. He is our heavenly Father who wants to be in right relationship with His earthly sons and daughters (you and me). God loves us just as a father loves his own children. But like any good parent, God teaches right vs. wrong and that choices have consequences. God's idea, His plan, and His choice is for man to be with Him forever in heaven. Pastor Creamer says heaven is a prepared place for a prepared people.

We Need a Reminder

People need to remember that another aspect of being made in God's image is that man was given the ability to make a decision and to choose one thing over another. Adam and Eve, were the first to misuse their ability to choose, and in so doing they introduced the knowledge of good and evil into the human race. God's original intention was for man to only experience good and to have no knowledge of evil, sin, or separation from God. Man was created to enjoy God always and to always be in close, loving, and peaceful fellowship with Him. But when the first humans chose to know good _and_ evil by eating from the tree of the knowledge of good and evil, man's experience became good _and_ evil. Choices always have consequences. My husband, Marshall, often says: "Make your choices, and then after that, your choices will make you!"

So people need a reminder that hell has been prepared for those who reject God and His plan for saving mankind. Matthew 25:41 says: _"Depart from me, ye cursed, into everlasting fire, prepared for the devil and his angels."_ Hell is for the devil and his demons and all who reject God willfully, consciously, and purposely. They need to understand that if they fail to choose God and His salvation plan through Christ, then they have rejected God and the ability to live with Him for eternity in heaven and have chosen their own eternal damnation and destruction.

Although it's not easy, let's keep telling them that hell is a place without God, without God's presence, without God's goodness, without God's attributes. Hell is depicted in the Bible as the lake of fire and has been described as a place where temperatures exceed 2,000 degrees! It has been described as a place where there is perpetual burning. People still have bodies, and even though those bodies are in enormous heat and fire, they do not burn up. They just keep burning in torment. Men will be able to feel the pain of that torment and will not be able to escape from it. Matthew 8:12 and Mark 9:44 tell us that there the worm dies not, and there will be weeping and gnashing of teeth. So if there will be weeping and gnashing of teeth, men will have bodies and they will feel the torment of the fires of hell. They will exist in that torment forever if they reject God while they live on the earth. Let's urge them to decide to choose Christ, to accept Him as Lord and Savior, and to join in right relationship with God through Christ. *"Jesus is the way, the truth, and the life and no man comes unto God the Father but by Him."* (John 14:6).

So dear friends, let's learn from Pastor Creamer, this general of the faith, that the most important aspect of Christian leadership and ministry is helping souls to be converted to the Lordship of Christ. You and I may not ever come close to the numbers of souls saved under her ministry of leadership, but let's continue to do our part being encouraged by I Corinthians 3:6 where the apostle Paul states: *"I have planted, Apollos watered; but God gave the increase."* Pastor's prayer continues to be that God will add to the church daily such as should be saved.

At times, Pastor Creamer would say that just one moment in His presence will be worth it all. It will be worth all the sorrows, pains, and vicissitudes of life. Can you imagine that? Just one moment in heaven with God will be worth it all! What a day of rejoicing that will be. When we all see Jesus, we *will* sing and *shout* the victory.

Heaven is the last stop and the final destination on this long, sometimes difficult journey of faith. With Christ as our Savior, we are on our way. He has saved us from the penalty of sin and won the victory of eternity with God in heaven. All who have placed their faith in Him, have heaven as their final destination. In John 14:3, Jesus said: *"I go to prepare a place for you . . . that where I am there you may be also."* Jesus has prepared the way for us to get to heaven one day. Heaven's beauty is apparent in the following description in Revelation 21:21-24:

> *"And the twelve gates were twelve pearls; every several gate was of one pearl: and the street of the city was pure gold, as it were transparent glass. And I saw no temple therein; for the Lord God Almighty and the Lamb are the temple of it. And the city had no need of the sun, neither of the moon, to shine in it: for the glory of God did lighten it, and the Lamb is the light thereof. And the nations of them which are saved shall walk in the light of it: and the kings of the earth do bring their glory and honour into it.*

Joy and happiness will be there. There'll be no more crying or sorrow there. *"And God shall wipe away all tears from their eyes; and there shall be no more death, neither sorrow, nor crying, neither shall there be any more: for the former things are passed away."* (Revelation 21:4)

Hallelujah, we're going to see the King of kings and the Lord of lords. We'll live for all eternity with the Prince of Peace who bought us and paid for us with His own life. We're heirs of God and joint heirs with Christ, and those who are in Christ and alive when He returns shall be caught up to meet Him in the air. What a day of rejoicing that will be! Our journey will be over, and our faith shall become sight. We shall behold Him, the Lamb of God to whom salvation and glory, honor and power belong. The majestic place of God's presence seems hard to fathom and harder to describe, yet we will behold Him and live with Him in glory. And just think, it will happen in a moment, in the twinkling of an eye:

> *"In a moment, in the twinkling of an eye, at the last trump: for the trumpet shall sound, and the dead shall be raised incorruptible, and we shall be changed. So when this corruptible shall have put on incorruption and this mortal shall have put on immortality, then shall be brought to pass the saying that is written, Death is swallowed up in victory."*
> I Cor. 15:52, 54

Heaven is our goal and our final resting place. It will be worth it all. Just one moment in God's presence will be worth it all! Don't stop, don't quit, and do not give up. Keep going. Keep pushing. Keep on pressing your way with the blessed hope in mind:

> *"For the Lord himself shall descend from heaven with a shout, with the voice of the archangel, and with the trump of God: and the dead in Christ shall rise first: Then we which are alive and remain shall be caught up together with them in the clouds to meet the Lord in the air: and so shall we ever be with the Lord."* I Thess. 4:16-17

We must go on. There'd be no greater lost, than not to see Jesus face to face. In the end, we win. We receive the pearl of great price, a crown of glory that fadeth not away, a white robe, a seat around the throne of God. Follow this beautiful example in the pages of this book Do what Pastor Creamer has done – live life for Jesus and you, too, will see Him one day.

All Is Well!

After all of these years in faithful ministry and service, Pastor Creamer's constant refrain is now that "all is well." These are the same words spoken by the Shunammite woman in II Kings Chapter 4. There, when Gehazi asked the Shunammite woman if something was wrong, her response was, *"Everything's fine."* II Kings 4:26 (Message Bible). Her son had just died, but she simply said, *"It is well."* II Kings 4:26 (KJV). A little while later, Elisha prayed for her son, and he came back to life! Pastor Creamer's faith in God parallels the faith of the Shunammite woman. Her faith in God was full of resurrection power. With that kind of faith in God, all *is* well.

Pastor encourages us not to let the "vicissitudes of life" stop us from getting to heaven. She'll say you can make it if you don't allow "the people" to get in your way.

She reminds you that sometimes you have to "move quickly," so you can avoid the "little foxes that spoil the vine." Pastor will encourage you to remember that "nothing's as precious as Jesus, nothing's as precious as He." She will encourage you not to worry but to "look at the birds" and see how well God takes care of them. When you're angry and want to fight back, Pastor Creamer will say "Don't fight, just praise Him," "be sweet," and "suck it up." She'll tell you not to expect to go to heaven "in a gravy train with biscuit wheels." She requires that we all work together because "many hands make light work" and "you can't be so heavenly minded that you're no earthly good." Pastor will encourage you to "clap those hands and tell God thank you" because "either you trust Him or you don't." She will help you along the way by encouraging you to come to church because "if you miss it, you missed it!" And you can count on Pastor Creamer to always pray for you and believe God for "miracles that cannot be denied" in your life.

Pastor Creamer has been an encourager of men's hearts and a builder of men's lives, always exhorting and admonishing everyone to look to Jesus Christ and live. She has founded and pastored an enduring ministry that has impacted generations with the hope of the gospel and the promise of Christ.

Be encouraged and inspired to press on, dear friends. God awaits you at the finish line when your journey is done. Pastor Creamer's prayer is that the God of all grace, after you have suffered a while will make you perfect, will establish you, will strengthen you, and will settle you. Pastor Creamer prays God's blessings upon your life, your ministry, and your own personal journey of faith. For the victory that will overcome this world and translate us into the kingdom of heaven – is and always shall be our enduring faith.

To God be all the glory, all the honor, and all the praise. We thank Him for all He has done through the life, the ministry, the sacrifice, and the leadership of Reverend Emma Loretta Curry Creamer who has left a permanent mark on the Christian faith as she continues to walk hand in hand with God.

A Profound Conclusion

Pastor Creamer is still faithfully serving in her role as Senior Pastor and Founder of the Cathedral of Fresh Fire. All the way from a broken piano, this year she will celebrate her 46th year in Christian ministry and service and her 22d year of pastoring!

It was her heartfelt desire to write this book. She said: "I want to leave something the people can have when I'm gone." She has given her whole life to others in the service of the Lord, and yet her desire is still to give more! At the completion of the final edit of this book, Pastor Creamer offered a perfect finale to this labor of love. The words I heard seemed to have come from a place very deep in her heart. They had traveled the distance from the place in her heart where she is intimate with God. The words she spoke were full of fidelity and sincerity, replete with clarity and truth. Her words signify the culmination of this work and the fulfillment of her purpose in writing this book.

On February 15, 2013, Pastor Creamer expressed her final thoughts to conclude this labor of love. Simply, quietly, and profoundly she summarized her life of sacrifice and service with the following the thought:

> "All I can say is Jesus is the best thing that ever happened to me. All I know is that Jesus is the best thing that ever happened to me. And if anyone should ever write my life story, for whatever reason, whatever reason there might be. He'll be there between each line of pain and glory. Jesus is the best thing that ever happened to me!"

LIFE LESSON 8
Heaven Is A Prepared Place For Prepared People

The ultimate goal of the Christian's journey of faith is to make it to heaven one glorious day. Nothing else matters more, and all else pales in comparison to this. That our faith achieves for us the victor's crown is what we live and die for. Heaven is our goal, and we want to make it in. It doesn't matter through which gate we enter – number one or two or twelve – we just want to get in. If it costs our lives, we've got to make it – make it to the city called Heaven.

Try not to be left behind. There'd be no greater loss. Refuse to draw back into perdition. Believe to the saving of your soul. It is imperative that we accomplish the en route goals in order to achieve the terminal goal. We must be born again. Let nothing and no one hinder you from reaching Heaven in the end. Include yourself in the list of people who may not get in your way. Allow no trickery from Satan to deceive or distract your focus from the place where Christ is seated at the right hand of God.

We'll never be good enough to qualify for entrance into Heaven. We cannot show up there through our own volition or strength. We must exchange our sin for the righteousness of Christ. We must be born again. Jesus shall forever be the only way there. Detours and shortcuts do not exist. Accept the finished work of Christ's substitutionary death, burial, and resurrection for you, and your way into Heaven is paid in full.

I hope and pray to meet you there some day.

THE VICE PRESIDENT

WASHINGTON

July 7, 2009

Pastor Emma L. Creamer
The Cathedral of Fresh Fire, Inc.
2300 Northeast Boulevard
Wilmington, DE 19802

Dear Pastor Creamer:

Please accept my most sincere congratulations on your 70th birthday and your 18th Pastoral Anniversary at the Cathedral of Fresh Fire. I commend you for a lifetime of unwavering faith and committed service.

I am confident Cathedral of Fresh Fire has inspired a great many people in our community and I wish you, as well as each member of the congregation, many more wonderful years of celebrating your faith.

Again, congratulations and I hope you take a moment to celebrate this latest milestone.

Sincerely,

Joseph R. Biden, Jr.

Proclamation from Vice President Joe Biden

Pastor Creamer has received numerous proclamations and awards from Bishops, Senators, Governors, Mayors, and other dignitaries

APPENDIX A

Milestones, Achievements
& Accomplishments
in the Life of Reverend Emma L. Creamer

Began playing piano in church	Age 7
Saved through new birth in Christ	Age 9
Baptized in the Holy Ghost	Age 12
Came to Delaware	Age 14
State youth leader	Age 15
Baptized in water	Age 16
Married Leon Creamer	Age 24
Daughter Yarah born	Age 25
Son LeAndre born	Age 27
Formed the Emma Creamer Singers	Age 27
Daughter Helena born	Age 28
Sang with Dorothy Norwood	1970
Passing of her natural mother, Mother Olive Curry	1973
Called to preach	1974
Became a COGIC National Evangelist	1982
Appointed administrative assistant	1983
Visited the Holy Land in Israel	1988
Hosted Vickie Wynans in concert	1989
Passing of her spiritual father, Rev. Ross B. Rainey	1991

Table continues on next page

Sued in court and won	1991
Ordained as pastor	1991
Founded the Cathedral of Fresh Fire, Inc.	1991
Founded first praise dancers in Delaware	1992
Led Exodus March to the Cathedral of Fresh Fire building	1994
Church rebuilding and restoration	1995
Cathedral of Fresh Fire church dedication	1997
Hosted Richard Smallwood in concert	1998
Became a charter campus of Chesapeake Bible College & Seminary	2003
Produced the original stage play, The Blood	2004
Wings of Healing television broadcast	2005
Produced the original stage play, Behold the Lamb	2008
Burned the $400,000 mortgage	2013
Memoirs published	2013
Number of souls led to Christ through her ministry	500+
Number of saints filled with Holy Spirit	300+
Number of believers water baptized	650+
Number of couples married	116
Number of deacons ordained	48
Number of ministers licensed	30
Number of elders ordained	27
Number of pastors ordained	5
Number of ministry departments	25
Number of years pastoring	22
Number of awards & proclamations	50+
Number of years in Christian ministry	46

APPENDIX B

A Chronology Of Inspired Preaching	
Original Sermons by Pastor Emma L. Creamer, 1990 — 2013	
Sermon Title	Scripture Reference
We Need A Reminder	Psalm 103:1-5
Feed Me Lord, I'm Hungry	Psalm 42:1, Luke 14:16-24
No Press No Life	II Corinthians 4:1
Hold On To What You Have In Christ	Revelation 3:11
The Same Spirit	Philippians 2:5
Love Lifted Me	I John 4:10, I Corinthians 13:13
He's That Kind of Friend	Proverbs 18:24
Hold On To What You've Got	Galatians 5:1
Press On	Philippians 3:13-14
God's Got A Blessing For You	John 5:5-6
Make Me Better	Psalm 57:7
Don't Take Thy Spirit	Zechariah 4:6 Psalm 51:11
Look at the Birds	Matthew 6:25-33
What Will A Man Give In Exchange For His Soul?	Mark 8:34-38
To Me, He Is Precious	I Peter 2:7
Wait For Your Change—It's Coming	Job 14:14
When Your Night Comes	John 9:4
Blow Wind Blow	Ezekiel 37:7
More Than Enough	Judges 6:1-8
My Season, My Time	Ecclesiastes 3:1-15
Lord Send Me, I'll Go	Isaiah 6:1-8
Urban Promise	Acts 2:33
Take Me Back	Revelation 2:5
Making It On Broken Pieces	Acts 27:31-44
Virtuous Women Magnifying God	Ephesians 4:3

Continued on next page

On the Left Hand Where God Doth Work	Job 23:9
What Do You Do When Your Brook Dries Up?	I Kings 17:1-7
God's Not Through With Me Yet	Luke 22:31-32
At the End, We Win in 2010	Joel 2:28, 32
Wilt Thou Be Made Whole?	I John 5:1-8
What Are You Worth?	Jeremiah 13:1-11
I Want That Anointing	II Kings 2:1-11
The Giants Keep Coming	I Samuel 17:32-51
Follow On To Know Him	Hosea 6:1-3
We've Been Touched by the Fire	Acts 2:1-8
An Honest Ministry	II Corintians 4:4-5
Thank You, Lord	Luke 17:11-16
First Things First	Matthew 6:33
Old Things Are Passed Away	II Corinthians 5:14-21
We Need A Touch From Jesus	John 9:1-6
Blizzards of Trouble	II Corinthians 6:3-10
Let's Get Along	Psalm 133
A Blessing Is Promised	Deuteronomy 23:23
Heaven	II Corinthians 5:1, 12:2
Lord Cover Us With Your Blood	Leviticus 17:11 Exodus 12:13
Joy in Affliction	Isaiah 9:6 Matthew 1:21
The Power of Unity: It Begins With U	I Corinthians 1:1-10
Let's Do It Together	Matthew 18:19-20
Strengthen Those Things That Remain	Revelation 3:1-6
The Christians' Hope	II Corinthians 5 Romans 8:28
The Word Became Flesh	John 1:1-14
It's Time to Take Your Vitamins	I Peter 2:1-3
Walking the Faith Walk	Romans 4:13-25
Seven Steps to Effective Prayer	James 5:13-18
The Prayerful Mother	I Samuel 1:4-11

Continued on next page

Weeping May Endure For A Night	Matthew 28:1-7
Hind's Feet in High Places	Habakkuk 3:19
Getting There	Matthew 11:28
The Pressure of Duty	John 9:1-6
Believe	Mark 9:23-24
The Lord My Shepherd	Psalm 23
A Fresh Wind Is Blowing	Acts 2:2
Go On	Joshua 1:1-5
Tear It Down	Ecclesiastes 3:3
It's My Season	Galatians 6:9

APPENDIX C

A Collection Of Pastor Creamer's Favorite Scriptures

Psalm 22:3

But thou art holy, O thou that inhabitest the praises of Israel

Psalm 55:6

And I said, Oh that I had wings like a dove! for then would I fly away, and be at rest.

Psalm 62:11

God hath spoken once; twice have I heard this; that power belongeth unto God.

Psalm 63:3-4

Because thy lovingkindness is better than life, my lips shall praise thee. Thus will I bless thee while I live: I will lift up my hands in thy name.

Psalm 71:17-18

O God, thou hast taught me from my youth: and hitherto have I declared thy wondrous works. Now also when I am old and greyheaded, O God, forsake me not; until I have shewed thy strength unto this generation, and thy power to every one that is to come.

Continued on next page

Proverbs 10:22

The blessing of the Lord, it maketh rich, and he addeth no sorrow with it.

Isaiah 58:1

Cry aloud, spare not, lift up thy voice like a trumpet, and shew my people their transgression, and the house of Jacob their sins.

Isaiah 59:1-2

Behold, the Lord's hand is not shortened, that it cannot save; neither his ear heavy, that it cannot hear: But your iniquities have separated between you and your God, and your sins have hid his face from you, that he will not hear.

Isaiah 61:3

To appoint unto them that mourn in Zion, to give unto them beauty for ashes, the oil of joy for mourning, the garment of praise for the spirit of heaviness; that they might be called trees of righteousness, the planting of the Lord, that he might be glorified.

Malachi 4:2

But unto you that fear my name shall the Sun of righteousness arise with healing in his wings; and ye shall go forth and grow up as calves of the stall.

Matthew 6:33

Seek ye first the kingdom of God and His righteousness and all these other things shall be added unto thee

Continued on next page

Mark 9:23

Jesus said unto him, canst thou believe, all things are possible to him that believeth.

Romans 8:26

Likewise the Spirit also helpeth our infirmities: for we know not what we should pray for as we ought: but the Spirit itself maketh intercession for us with groanings which cannot be uttered.

II Corinthians 4:8

We are troubled on every side, yet not distressed; we are perplexed, but not in despair;

Galatians 6:9

And let us not be weary in well doing: for in due season we shall reap, if we faint not.

Ephesians 6:11

Put on the whole armour of God, that ye may be able to stand against the wiles of the devil.

Philippians 3:10

That I may know him, and the power of his resurrection, and the fellowship of his sufferings, being made conformable unto his death;

Continued on next page

Philippians 3:13-14

Brethren, I count not myself to have apprehended: but this one thing I do, forgetting those things which are behind, and reaching forth unto those things which are before, I press toward the mark for the prize of the high calling of God in Christ Jesus.

Philippians 4:13

I can do all things through Christ which strengtheneth me.

James 1:5

If any of you lack wisdom, let him ask of God, that giveth to all men liberally, and upbraideth not; and it shall be given him.

APPENDIX D

A Memorable Ministry Of Music

In October 1974, while attending Doswell Temple Church of God in Christ, Dr. L Ramona Howard and I were sitting in the congregation when Bishop Doswell, asked this tall woman with beautiful grey hair to come to the front to sing a solo prior to him preaching. Evangelist Emma Creamer was her name, and she went to the piano, gave greetings and stated she was in bad voice due to a cold she had been fighting, but she would try to sing anyway. She opened her mouth and this anointed voice came out, the spirit of the Lord went through the congregation, and the Bishop could not preach because the spirit was so high. Dr. Howard said, "I am going to catch her as she is leaving," and she got her information. They began talking, and she found out Dr Howard could play the organ. We went with Evangelist Creamer to several engagements. At every service they would ask her to sing. One day we went to her house, and we rehearsed and Dr. Howard, Evangelist Emma Creamer, and I became the Emma Creamer Singers.

At that time her ministry was just taking off. Soon she was preaching two afternoon services in different states many times, almost every Sunday, and we were singing at every service. The people began to request recordings, and we evolved from cassettes to the albums. A recording was made of us for TV in Wilmington. They played that tape over and over, and sometimes it still comes on because of the request for the Emma Creamer Singers. Everyone was saying we had the authentic sound of traditional gospel seasoned with the Holy Ghost. The first album sold so quickly, and the requests were so numerous, a second album was recorded.

Albums were recorded at Virtue Recording Studio 614 N. Broad Street. Phila., PA. There Is Nothing As Precious As Jesus was the first album. The artwork and cover design were done by Cedric D. Crawford.   *Written by Elder Delnora Ann Roberts*

Pastor Creamer's Original Recordings/Albums*

Call on Jesus, He Will Answer*

Emma Creamer, Delnora Roberts, Tammy Lindsay, Dr. L. Ramona Howard

1. Call on Jesus
2. Where Jesus Is
3. I Came to the Garden Alone
4. Bless Me Lord
5. I'm Glad the Lord Chose Me
6. Nothing But the Blessed
7. In Short, He's My Everything
8. He Keeps Doing Great Things

There Is Nothing As Precious Jesus*

Emma Creamer, Tammy Lindsay, Delnora Roberts

1. There Is Nothing As Precious As Jesus
2. He's Done So Much For Me
3. If You Put Your Trust in Jesus
4. There Is No Way
5. Standing on the Promises
6. I'm So Glad I'm Saved Today
7. Walk in the Light

Move With the Spirit*

Emma Creamer

1. Move With the Spirit
2. He Has A Way
3. God's Truth Is Marching On
4. Old Time Religion
5. Bless the Name of Jesus
6. You're Coming Back, Jesus
7. When He Died
8. He's A Way Maker
9. Precious Lord
10. Ole Zion

A Few of the Gospel Greats She Sang With

Dorothy Norwood

Shirley Ceasar

Roger Roberts Singers

Cloud-Davis Specials

Some Gospel Greats She Has Hosted

Vickie Wynans

Williams Brothers

Richard Smallwood

The Mighty Aires

Some of Pastor Creamer's Most Memorable Renditions

Always Remember Jesus	Gentle Holy Spirit
Bless the Lord, Oh My Soul	I Don't Know What You've Come To Do
Blessings, Glory and Honor	Jesus, I'll Never Forget
Emmanuel, Our God Is With Us	Praise Him & Lift Him Up
You Are the Holy One	Precious Jesus, How I Love Thee
God Is Great & Greatly To Be Praised	Something in My Heart Like a Stream Running Down
He Keeps on Doing Great Things	Spirit of the Living God, Fall Fresh On Me
I Thank You, Jesus	Surely the Presence
If You Don't Praise Him, Well Then	That's Why My Heart Is Filled With Praise
Jesus Is the Best Thing That Ever Happened To Me	Trust in the Lord
Jesus, Precious King	We Bring the Sacrifice of Praise
Surely The Presence of the Lord	What More Can He Do
The Gloria Patri	Where Jesus Is 'Tis Heaven There
There's A Storm Out on the Ocean	Yes, Lord
When Was Jesus Born?	You're My Healing Jesus
Where Could I Go But to the Lord	Zion is Calling Me to a Higher Place of Praise
I Must Go On	Call on Jesus, He Will Answer Prayer

*** Many of Pastor Creamer's recordings are available on cd by calling 302-764-3344*

THE ROGER ROBERTS SINGERS

Business Management
Mrs. Senora Hyland
1004 Lombard St.
Wilmington, Del.
Phone 652-7171

Emma Creamer with the Roger Roberts
Singers
*"Come before His presence with
singing"*

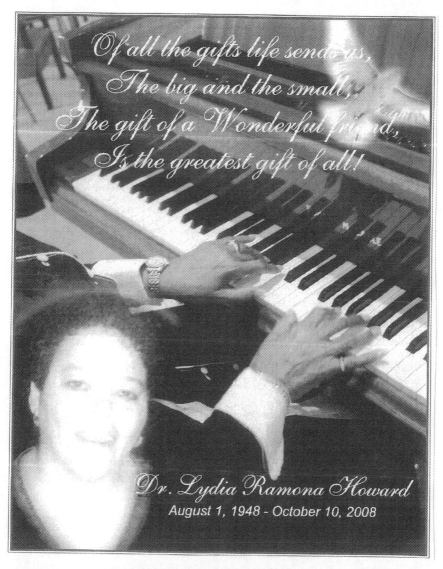

Of all the gifts life sends us,
The big and the small,
The gift of a Wonderful friend,
Is the greatest gift of all!

Dr. Lydia Ramona Howard
August 1, 1948 - October 10, 2008

Pastor Creamer and the late Dr. L. Ramona
Howard
"O magnify the Lord with me!"

APPENDIX E

A Collection Of Pastor Creamer's Inspirational Quotes

You better see this thing!	Move quickly!	Look at you lookin' at me!
Give God excellence	The viccissitudes of life!	The people!
I'm so blessed I don't know what to do with myself	You have to make straight paths for your feet	Some think they can go to heaven in a gravy train with biscuit wheels
Where Jesus is, 'tis heaven there	Miracles that cannot be denied	Step up!
Suck it up!	Watch me!	Don't be slothful
Don't give a good bucket of milk and then kick it over	You can't be so heavenly minded that you're no earthly good	Clap those hands and tell God thank you!
Say what I'm saying!	Be sweet	All is well
Either you trust Him or you don't	Come on and say yes in here	All God wants is a "yes"
Don't use my God like a spare tire or a fire escape	You have six months to mind your business and six months to leave mine alone	Don't give me flowers when I'm dead, give them to me when I can smell them

Continued on next page

If you missed it, you missed it	It's the little foxes that spoil the vine	And they sang a song and went out
The blood make whole, the blood deliver, the blood set free	If you be willing and obedient, you shall eat the good of the land	Jesus is the best thing that ever happened to me
If you can be on time for your job, you can be on time for God	Where there's unity, there's strength, where there's strength, there's power, where there's power, there's change	Working for Jesus may not pay much, but the retirement plan is out of this world
Everybody who comes with you, can't go with you	If nobody is following you, you're just a man taking a walk.	God is speaking
Many hands make light work	Prayer is the key and faith unlocks the door	Set the table and if they're hungry, they'll come and eat
Sheep beget sheep	Heaven is a prepared place for a prepared people	He's good *to me*!
Why buy the cow, when you can get the milk for free?	If everyone in my church was just like me, what kind of church would my church be?	We can fill a whole 'nother world with what you don't know

APPENDIX F

A Church of Leaders

Department (or Position)	President
Associate Pastor	Elder Danny Dover
Children's Church	Missionary Sharon Dover
Christian Education	Co-Pastor Helena Creamer
Choirs/Praise Team	Minister of Music Charles Finney
Church Administrator	Minister Bernadine McCants
Church Secretary	Elder Carolyn Martin-Pettaway
Co-Pastor	Elder Helena Creamer
Culinary Staff	Missionary Brenda Davis
Dance Ministry	Sister Tabita Ares (Artistic Director)
Deacons	Deacon Gary Marshall
Elders	Senior Pastor Emma Creamer
Evangelists	Co-Pastor Helena Creamer
Health & Wellness Ministry	Elder Carolyn Peak
Helping Hand Outreach	Missionary Brenda Davis
Marriage Ministry	Elder Barbara Washington
Men's Ministry	Associate Pastor Danny Dover
Ministers	Co-Pastor Helena Creamer
Ministry Coordinator	Elder Jacquelyn Rivers
Missionaries	Missionary Brenda Davis
Musicians	Minister of Music Charles Finney
Mothers	Mother Rosetta Finney
New Members' Ministry	Elder Jacquelyn Rivers
Nurses	Sister Brandi English
Pastor's Adjutant	Evangelist JaDean Mills
Pastor's Support Team	Minister Deborah Bryant
Security Team	Brother Ronald Johnson
Sunday School	Elder Roslyn Whitehurst
Trustees	Elder Larry DeJarnette
Ushers	Deacon Eric Evans
Women's Ministry	Minister Vivian Staples
Youth Ministry	Youth Pastor Vaughn Watson

APPENDIX G

Rev. Emma L. Creamer
Pastor & Founder

The Cathedral of Fresh Fire, Inc.
"Where Pentecostal Flames Are Always Burning"
2300 Northeast Boulevard, Wilmington, DE 19802
302-764-3344 302-764-2177 fax
302-764-1063 or 1-888-451-FIRE prayer lines
www.cathedraloffreshfire.com

Sunday School   9:00 a.m.
Sunday Morning Worship   10:00 a.m.
Monday Night Prayer   7:00 p.m.
Youth Sunday Every 3d Sunday

Mission Statement

To create a perpetual environment which fosters spiritual education, deliverance, growth and maturity as prescribed in the Holy Bible; ALWAYS showing the life changing power of God.

APPENDIX H

Statement of Faith

We believe the Bible to be the inspired and only infallible word of God.

We believe that there is only one God, eternally existent in three persons, God the Father, God the Son, and God the Holy Spirit.

We believe in the blessed hope, which is the rapture of the church of God, which is in Christ at His return.

We believe that the only means of being cleansed from sin is through repentance, faith in the precious blood of Jesus Christ, and being baptized in water.

Continued on next page

We believe that regeneration by the Holy Spirit is absolutely essential for personal salvation.

We believe that the redemptive work of Christ on the cross provides healing for the human body in answer to believing prayer.

We believe that the baptism of the Holy Ghost, according to Acts 2:4 is given to believers who ask for it.

We believe in the sanctifying power of the Holy Spirit, by whose indwelling the Christian is enabled to live a holy and separated life in this present world. Amen.

My Amazing Journey of Faith!

Rev. Ross B. Rainey

Mother Olive Curry "Mom"

Reverend Ross B. Rainey and Mother Olive Curry
Pastor Emma Loretta Curry Creamer
Psalm 71:17-18

O God, thou hast taught me from my youth: and hitherto have I declared thy wondrous works. Now also when I am old and greyheaded, O God, forsake me not; until I have shewed thy strength unto this generation, and thy power to every one that is to come.

BIBLIOGRAPHY

Bible References*

Holy Bible, New King James Version, Thomas Nelson Publishers Inc., Nashville, TN, 1982.

King James Quick Reference Bible, Authorized King James, Thomas Nelson Publishers Inc., Nashville, TN, 2000.

Peterson, Eugene H., The Message/Remix, The Bible in Contemporary Language, Navpress, Colorado Springs, Colorado, 2003

Other References

Chambers, Oswald, My Utmost For His Highest, Selections for the Year, p, 56, Discovery House Publishers, Grand Rapids, Michigan, 1935.

Church, Leslie F., Matthew Henry's Commentary In One Volume, p. 197, Zondervan Publishing House, Grand Rapids, Michigan, 1961

Edwards, Jonathan, Classic Sermons on Praise, Praise, One of the Chief Employments of Heaven, p. 45, Compiled by Warren W. Wiersbe, Hendrickson Publishers, Inc., Grand Rapids, Michigan, 1994.

Eims, LeRoy, Be the Leader You Were Meant to Be, p. 21, Chariot Victor Publishing, Colorado Springs, Colorado, 1996.

Peak, Carolyn, <u>Our God Is An Awesome God</u>, The Holy Spirit: An Introductory Study, pp. 36-37, The Cathedral School of the Bible, Wilmington, Delaware, 2004.

Whitehurst, Roslyn, <u>Pray: With Purpose and Power</u>, p. 9, The Cathedral School of the Bible, Wilmington, Delaware, 2004.